Documentary Film and Radical Psychiatry

Des O'Rawe

Documentary Film and Radical Psychiatry

palgrave
macmillan

Des O'Rawe
School of Arts, English and Languages
Queen's University Belfast
Belfast, UK

ISBN 978-3-031-74230-9   ISBN 978-3-031-74231-6   (eBook)
https://doi.org/10.1007/978-3-031-74231-6

Cover illustration: Pattern © Melisa Hasan

This Palgrave Macmillan imprint is published by the registered company Springer Nature
Switzerland AG.
The registered company address is: Gewerbestrasse 11, 6330 Cham, Switzerland

If disposing of this product, please recycle the paper.

PREFACE

This book is primarily intended for anyone with an interest in documentary film studies, and especially the transformations associated with the production of documentaries during the long 1960s. Hopefully, it might also be of some use to researchers and teachers working across interdisciplinary areas such as health and medical humanities, disability studies, and comparative cinema and screen studies.

In scope and argument, it inevitably focuses on the relations between documentary and radical psychiatry within a predominantly Western context. It is true that some psychiatrists—influenced by the writings of figures like Albert Memmi, Paulo Freire, Octave Mannoni, and Frantz Fanon—wanted to more actively "decolonize madness" but in applying essentially Western categories and cultural assumptions to historically colonised societies, they risked becoming complicit in a neo-colonial enterprise rather than an anti-colonial one. This is an important issue in the history and politics of documentary film (especially, given the "humanitarian" role often attributed to ethnographic filmmaking) and to do it justice would require a dedicated study involving extensive archival and transcultural research. In general, documentary filmmaking on the relations between radical psychiatry and anti-colonialism is rare enough, and even contemporary films about Fanon—for example, *Concerning Violence* (Goran Hugo Olsson, 2014) or Isaac Julien's *Frantz Fanon: Black Skin, White Mask* (1995)—will tend to focus on biography and political theory, rather than psychiatry and Fanon's relationship with institutional psychotherapy. That all said, *Frantz Fanon: Memories from the Asylum*, a 2002 documentary directed by the Algerian filmmaker, Abdenour Zahzah, is a notable exception in this regard.

For social historians of the long 1960s, the relationship between radical psychiatry and feminism is similarly important, although again there are relatively few independent documentaries from that era on the work of feminist "anti-psychiatry" campaigners in the US, like Hogie Wyckoff, Phyllis Chesler, Judi Chamberlin, or within a more European context, figures such as Françoise Dolto, Juliette Favez-Boutonnier, or Antionette Fouque and the Psychanalyse et Politique group. Maud Mannoni and the special education project she established at Bonneuil-sur-Marne was the subject of two documentaries, both directed by Guy Seligmann (*Vivre à Bonneuil*, 1974; *Secrète Enfance*, 1977), and her associations with Jacques Lacan, the Clinic of La Borde, Fernaud Deligny, and even RD Laing and David Cooper, created opportunities for dialogue between alternative pedagogy, institutional psychotherapy, and "anti-psychiatry". Although reference is made to these connections in this book, a more wide-ranging discussion would distract from its ostensible focus on feature documentaries, rather than shorter-form interview-based productions for television, education or training purposes. Furthermore, as the 1970s unfolded many feminist therapists and theorists (including Dolto, Mannoni, Julia Kristeva, Luce Irigaray, Juliet Mitchell, and Jessica Benjamin, for example) became more interested in exploring the possibilities presented by psychoanalytic feminism than in advocating for, or against, radical psychiatry. The commitment to filmmaking within this intellectual and activist context was also increasingly expressed through avant-garde, counter-cinema forms and practices, as in the case of figures like Laura Mulvey (*Riddles of the Sphinx*, 1974), Carola Klein (*Mirror Phase*, 1978), Dore O (*Kaskara*, 1974), and the Jay Street Collective's *Sigmund Freud's Dora: A Case of Mistaken Identity* (1979).

Yvonne Rainer's *Journeys from Berlin/1971* (1980) also belongs to that tradition, and its references to the Red Army Faction (RAF)/Baader-Meinhof Group might implicitly accuse this book of being insufficiently critical of radical psychiatry; especially in relation to its more extremist elements, such as the Socialist Patients' Collective (SPK/Sozialistisches Patientenkollektiv). Based in Heidelberg, and founded by Wolfgang Huber in 1970, the SPK counted amongst its ranks individuals closely associated with the RAF. However, in disseminating its political demands, the SPK preferred publishing articles, pamphlets, and manifestos rather than producing documentary films. Similarly, filmmaking was not the preferred, or even a very practical, mode of communication for intercultural and "anti-psychiatry" movements in Latin America, especially in Mexico, Argentina, and El Salvador, where the work and writings of figures like Cooper, Guattari, Franco Basaglia and Franca Ongara Basaglia, Thomas Szasz, Marie Langer, and Robert Castel directly influenced organisations such as the Red Latinoamericana de Alternativas a la Psiquiatría, or the Federación Argentina de Psiquiatras (FAP).

All of this might seem a somewhat long-winded way of pointing out that this book has not been written by a historian or anthropologist of psychiatry. The critical practice adopted throughout is attentive to relevant contexts without unduly privileging them over questions of cinematic form, structure, intention, and method. Just because a documentary filmmaker's motives are good does not necessarily mean they are pure, any more than because something is factual means it is true. All documentary filmmakers (whether they like to admit it or not) are involved in negotiating these paradoxes: to research, write, frame, shoot, edit, and produce a documentary film is to enter into realms of creativity, imagination, choice and subjectivity. Hopefully, what follows is sympathetic to filmmakers who embrace this reality and who do not presume to possess "the truth", and who, in their filmmaking, recognise an opportunity to discover something about themselves as well as radical psychiatry and the politics of mental illness.

Belfast, UK   Des O'Rawe

Acknowledgements

This book began life while I was co-organising a Wellcome Trust-funded *Framing Trauma* colloquium at Belfast Metropolitan Arts Centre (MAC), with Ciaran Mulholland. I am also grateful to Bonnie Evans and Janet Harbord, who invited me to participate in the *Film, Observation and Mind* symposium, which took place in 2020 as part of the Autism Through Cinema project. My research and writing was also supported by a timely sabbatical fellowship at the Senator George J. Mitchell Institute for Global Peace, Security and Justice at Queen's University, Belfast. Versions of parts from this book have appeared in print as follows: *History of the Human Sciences* 37 (2) and *Journal of Aesthetics and Culture* 11 (1).

I would like especially to thank Francis Hagan, Rod Stoneman, Stefano Baschiera, Peter Kane, and Mark Phelan for advice, criticism, translations, and misadventures along the way.

My greatest debt of gratitude is to Deirdre, not least somehow in convincing me that a new Golden Retriever in the hall need not be a sombre enemy of writing.

CONTENTS

Contents

ABOUT THE AUTHOR

Des O'Rawe is a senior lecturer in Film Studies at Queen's University Belfast, UK, where he is also a research fellow at the Senator George J. Mitchell Institute for Global Peace, Security and Justice. He is the author of *Regarding the Real: Cinema, Documentary, and the Visual Arts* (Manchester University Press, 2016), the co-editor of *Post-Conflict Performance, Film, and Visual Arts: Cities of Memory* (Palgrave, 2016) and he has written widely about the cinema for various journals and collections.

LIST OF FIGURES

CHAPTER 1

Introduction

Abstract The introductory chapter presents contextual background to the book. It begins by discussing the impact of the long 1960s on prevailing attitudes to mental illness, and the various important new studies on psychiatric institutions, schizophrenia, sexuality, and social psychology that attracted a general as well as specialised readership at that time. It then considers how the field of documentary filmmaking was also undergoing its own transformations in the post-war period. Consistent with the contemporary culture of political activism, documentary filmmaking became increasingly instrumental in struggles for social justice, and cultural representation. Inevitably, this activism often involved supporting specific mental healthcare reforms and promoting the development of progressive therapeutic communities.

Keywords Documentary • Radical psychiatry • The Long 1960s • Cinema • Trauma • Representation

As the popular modern artform most strongly associated with representations of psychosis it is hardly surprising that the cinema has derived so much of its dramatic content and critical theory from psychiatric discourse. Documentary film has played a key role in this relationship, and even in the early cinema era psychiatric and psychological documentaries were as

D. O'Rawe, *Documentary Film and Radical Psychiatry*, https://doi.org/10.1007/978-3-031-74231-6_1

notable for the relative sophistication of their rhetorical structures as for their dissemination of medical knowledge (Evans 2024, 12–40; Stastny 1998, 68–90). Nowadays, the advent of digital technologies, streaming platforms, online and in-person festivals has resulted in a seemingly exponential increase in the number of short and feature documentary productions dealing with contemporary mental healthcare provision, controversial psychiatric treatments, depression, and schizophrenia (Vallejo 2020, 77–100; O'Sullivan 2017, 151–57). Regardless of its array of observational techniques, evidential claims and ethical concerns, however, the documentary remains especially tested by the task of representing psychiatric subjects and institutions: Do the stylistic conventions and modes of address associated with documentary filmmaking, for example, serve to reinforce stereotypical images of "madness", legitimizing the authority of psychiatry by being complicit in the very prejudices the filmmakers are claiming to subvert? Does the presence of the camera—even in seemingly democratic psychiatric communities—inevitably encourage a performance of identities rather than capturing the realities of life and relationships in that environment? Even if explicitly supportive of certain alternative approaches to understanding and treating mental illness, is it ever possible to develop a documentary film practice capable of articulating advocacy without courting sentimentality and inauthenticity?

This book explores these issues by engaging with the work of documentary filmmakers who have aligned their methods and social commitments with a wider critique of conventional psychiatric medicine. It considers the relations between documentary film and radical psychiatry during the long 1960s, although occasionally that time-frame has been extended to accommodate comparative reference to more recent films on this subject. This was a definitive epoch in both the histories of documentary film and psychiatry, a period of profound epistemic upheaval that inaugurated a new politics of the counter-culture, amidst Cold War antagonisms and global processes of decolonisation. Within this context, the term "radical psychiatry" is understood throughout this study in its broad sense, i.e. encompassing a variety of cognate counter-cultural tendencies, such as: anti-psychiatry, critical psychiatry, post-psychiatry, radical therapy, institutional psychotherapy, schizoanalysis, and psychedelic psychiatry. In this regard, the book is sympathetic towards those filmmakers who, in the words of Serge Daney, understand that "quash[ing] the overwhelming impact of the word 'madness' [and] the normative violence of psychiatric nosography [...] consists not in relocating [...] but in relentlessly dynamiting both the word and the thing, in blowing up the material cage of madness, by connecting the camera to another space, one that is even less feasible, of all the real experiences that rescind the 'wall of the asylum'" (Daney 2022, 180–181).

Throughout the post-war period, psychiatrists, psychologists, and other mental healthcare workers came under increasing pressure to understand mental illness as a sociological phenomenon rather than a biomedical fact, a consequence of capitalism and its peculiar structural formations rather than the product of diagnosable neurochemical and emotional disorders. From this perspective, the mental hospital—or asylum—was increasingly viewed as a locus of symbolic power rather than therapeutic care, staffed by willing or deluded accomplices in the violence of classifying individuals as being "schizophrenic", "sociopathic", "depressive", "neurotic", or however so defined by the *Diagnostic and Statistical Manual of Disorders* (i.e. DSM-1 (1952), and DSM-2 (1968). Between 1960–62, a remarkable number of important, if methodologically diverse, critical studies on psychiatry and mental illness were published: Michel Foucault's *Madness and Civilization* (1961); Joseph Gabel's *False Consciousness* (1962); Alan Watts's *The Joyous Cosmology* (1962); Erving Goffman's *Asylums* (1961); R.D. Laing's *The Divided Self: An Existential Study in Sanity and Madness* (1960) and *The Self and Others* (1961); Martti Siirala's *The Schizophrenia of the Individual and Society* (1961); Frantz Fanon's The *Wretched of the Earth/ Les Damnés de la Terre* (1961, with its first English translation published in 1963); Harry Stack Sullivan's posthumously published papers, *Schizophrenia as a Human Process* (1962); and Thomas Szasz's bestselling *The Myth of Mental Illness: Foundations of a Theory of Personal Conduct* (1961); as was Gregory Bateson's early research on the family and the structural origins of schizophrenia. The year 1961 also "marked the slow beginning of the Basaglian revolution in Gorizia", which sought to democratize Italian psychiatric care by dismantling that country's farrago of decrepit mental hospitals (Foot 2015, 50). Opposition to mainstream psychiatry and psychology was also encouraged at this time by the New Left, with writings by figures such as Antonio Gramsci, Ernst Bloch, Eric Fromm, and Herbert Marcuse offering "re-readings" of classical Marxism through the lens of culture, ideas, being and consciousness—a reorientation that was to prove especially influential within the ranks of the more activist anti-psychiatry movement.

Meanwhile, the growing culture of scepticism towards traditional psychiatric authorities and treatments was also being reflected in contemporary popular culture through, for example, bestselling novels such as Richard Condon's *The Manchurian Candidate* (1959), *Shock Treatment* (Winfred van Atta, 1961), *Catch-22* (Joseph Heller, 1961), and Ken Kesey's *One Flew Over the Cuckoo's Nest* (1962), all of which were subsequently adapted into major Hollywood films (in 1962, 1964, 1970, and 1975 respectively). Sam Fuller's classic B-movie, *Shock Corridor* (1963), tapped into Cold War preoccupations with the effects of "combat stress", psychopharmacology, paranoia, and the general disquiet caused by Stanley Milgram's *Obedience* (1962), which comprised documentary recordings of his controversial psychological experiments (which had been inspired by the trial of Adolf Eichmann in Jerusalem). Interestingly, Fuller's attempts to provide a realistic portrayal of how patients were being treated in American psychiatric hospitals fell afoul of the censors: "At the beginning of *Shock Corridor*, I wanted to show [...] naked men and women chained together on benches in a long corridor, sitting in their own filth [...] The Hollywood censor board refused me permission. I produced photographs from several mental institutions showing this was no fabrication and they still said no" (Fuller 2012, 74). As a veteran of the Second World War, who had participated in the 1945 liberation of the Falkenau camps in Czechoslovakia, Fuller was especially alert to the "concentrationary" connotations of such images, and their potential to ask how the so-called Free World justified incarcerating so many of its most vulnerable citizens.

This contradiction also resonates through Frederick Wiseman's still controversial documentary, *Titicut Follies* (1967); which itself became famously entangled in complicated court cases, with public screenings effectively banned by the Massachusetts Supreme Court until the mid-1990s. The film observes the institutional processes at the Bridgewater State Hospital for the Criminally Insane, and the reality it exposes is one of a hospital/prison largely comprised of desolate patients/inmates being subjected to routine degradation and bureaucratic indifference. Footage of patients being made to strip, or being force-fed, demeaned and infantilised within the American judicio-psychiatric panopticon was a powerful indictment of prevailing attitudes to the treatment of mental illness there, and elsewhere. While clearly an important work in any study of the relations between documentary and psychiatry, *Titicut Follies* primarily exposes the failures of a system wedded to traditional prejudices around mental illness (and, in this case, resistant to the Kennedy Administration's 1963 Community Mental Health Act (CMHA)). Although Wiseman tended to eschew the journalistic approach of the classic Direct Cinema style (importantly, he had originally been trained as a lawyer rather than a journalist), *Titicut Follies* does confront its audience—when the film was permitted to have one—with disturbing documentary evidence about how such facilities were being managed, and the behaviour of many who worked there.

While not itself concerned with the emergence of alternative approaches to psychiatric care, *Titicut Follies* still offers an instructive documentary depiction of the kinds of institutional cultures and healthcare regimes that growing numbers of social activists wanted to abolish in the 1960s and 1970s. The film's history—and Wiseman's distinctive editing style—has made it a key work in discussions about documentary ethics and the filming of psychiatric patients (Kahana 2008, 222–37). Combining an unflinching commitment to social reality with highly expressive—modernist, even—techniques, *Titicut Follies* also continues to divide opinion over whether its method is subversive or transgressive, ethnographic or pornographic. Even amongst those documentary filmmakers generally appreciative of Wiseman's work, there is a noticeably ambivalent attitude towards the film. According to Albert Maysles, for example: "*Titicut Follies* was trying to put down the system, but [Wiseman] hurt the very people he meant to be protecting: the patients, the way he filmed them, with very little humanity" (McElhaney 2009, 160). In its subject matter, visual style and "'day in the life' [narrative] structure, and the broader metaphorical movement from life to death" (Grimshaw and Ravetz 2009, 47), *Titicut Follies* is still a touchstone when examining films such as Allan King's *Warrendale* (1967), Mario Ruspoli's *A Look at Madness/Regard sur la folie* (1962), or *San Clemente* (1982, Raymond Depardon and Sophie Ristelhueber), especially in relation to how these documentaries represent institutional relations between carers and patients. Arguably, whereas Wiseman invariably maintains a detached relationship to his subjects, King and Ruspoli's documentary methods afford the filmmaker more scope for interaction and social advocacy.

As indicated above, the corpus of documentaries dealing with influential figures, theories, and practices related to radical psychiatry is varied and predominantly European or North American, especially within the context of the long 1960s (Joice 2022, 11–15). Recent scholarship in this area has tended to stress the role of documentary in supporting specific mental healthcare reforms and promoting the development of progressive therapeutic communities within a given Western society and culture. In the case of Italy, for example, the influence of the Basaglias in the production of films such as *The Open Door/La porta aperta* (1968, Michele Gandin), *The Gardens of Abel/I Giardini di Abele* (Sergio Zavoli, 1969), *Mad People to Untie/Nessuno o tutti—Matti da slegare* (Silvano Agosti, et al. 1975), *The Poetry of Madness/Follia come poesia* (Lina Mangiacapre, 1979), and even *San Clemente* has been discussed quite extensively (e.g. Foot 2015, 218–223; Forgacs 2014, 243–250; Emerson 2021). Similarly, there is a growing body of scholarship available examining the relations between the French experience of radical therapeutic approaches to mental illness, neurodiversity, complex trauma and documentary film, especially regarding the remarkable career (and filmmaking activities) of Fernand Deligny (Witt 2022; Marlon 2022). Other studies have focussed on documentaries about the institutional psychotherapy movement in post-war France, looking at how the politics and philosophy of radical psychiatry intersects with the aesthetics of the documentary image (Bandosz 2021); these studies have also highlighted the particular significance of filmmaking about—and within—the famous Clinic of La Borde. Within a British context, meanwhile, the persona and practices of R.D. Laing (and the Philadelphia Association) have been the subject of various observational (e.g. *Asylum* (Peter Robinson, 1972)), expository (e.g. *Schizophrenia: A Disease or Just a Label?/Schizofreni: en sjukdom eller bara en etikett* (1970, Lars Wallin)), and experimental documentaries (David Lamelus' *Reading Film from Knots by R.D. Laing* (1970), and more recently, Luke Fowler's work); as well as realistic docu-dramatizations directly influenced by Laingian thinking (e.g. the Ken Loach-directed films, *In Two Minds* (1967) and *Family Life* (1971)). In one sense, this is not surprising given Laing's subsequent "celebrity" status and the range of his own writings and media appearances. In another sense, however, as Tim Snelson has pointed out, although these contemporary films "intensif[ied] an adversarial relationship between 'rebel' anti-psychiatrists and hard-line behaviourists [...], the wider psychiatric field largely welcomed the films' contributions to mental health awareness and used the publicity to counter the idea of a 'battle' within the profession" (Snelson 2021, 55).

In exploring how these and other documentaries negotiate the complexities of such radical and often highly controversial approaches to mental illness, the following chapters give due consideration to the influence of wider historical, structural, and autobiographical factors, and take their cue from the reality that, as Susan Sontag memorably put it: "In every society, the definitions of sanity and madness are arbitrary - are, in the largest sense, political" (Sontag 1988, lv). Essentially, the book argues that documentary filmmaking can offer critical perspectives on prevailing policies, treatments, and attitudes within the psychiatric profession, as well as contributing to a critique of how normative modes of being are constructed across the mainstream media and within popular culture. In their investigations into these issues, documentaries should also question the ethnographic and observational integrity of the documentary form itself, especially when it adopts diaristic, interactive, socially-engaged, and advocatory methods to represent mental healthcare issues in a supposedly humanitarian light. The goal of intelligent, democratic engagement with psychiatry through the medium of documentary film is a significant legacy of the long 1960s.

Chapter 2 begins this discussion by looking at documentaries dealing with the practices and persona of R.D. Laing, and how these films contribute to understanding the tensions in Laing's career between psychiatry and celebrity, controversy and caricature. Generally speaking, Laing has remained ever-present in the popular imagination through works like Graeme Macrae Burnet's critically-acclaimed novel, *Case-Study* (2022), for example; or the feature film *Mad to Be Normal* (Robert Mullan, 2017); or Patrick Marmion's 2015 play, *The Divided Laing: or The Two Ronnies*; and Luke Fowler's Turner-prize short-listed collage of archival images and experimental soundscapes, *All Divided Selves* (2011, 93 min.). In addition to discussing the series of Laing documentaries made by Canadian filmmaker, Peter Robinson, in the early 1970s (especially, *Asylum* (1970) and *R.D. Laing in the USA* (1973, 23 min)), the chapter examines other documentaries before concluding with a discussion of Fowler's work on Laing, and images of Laing.

Moving from the mainly British context of Laing's radical psychiatry, Chap. 3 examines how various European documentaries responded to Italy's experiences of deinstitutionalisation in the 1960s and 1970s, and how filmmakers actively engaged with the "politics of madness" associated with the work of Franco Basaglia. This discussion culminates in an analysis of *San Clemente*—a film that offers both an important insight into the scale of Basaglia's task, and Raymond Depardon's own problematic interest in the treatment and mistreatment of the psychiatric subject in contemporary France. Chapter Three also discusses the connections between documentary film and the institutional psychotherapy movement in France, especially as it was practiced in the psychiatric hospital of St-Alban, in Lozère, in the immediate post-war period, and at La Borde Clinic, in the Loire Valley. Central to this part of the discussion is Mario Ruspoli's *A Look at Madness*, which takes as its subject the experimental approaches developed by figures such as François Tosquelles at Saint-Alban. As the influence of institutional psychotherapy spread, it also became associated with La Borde, and figures such as Jean Oury, Roger Gentis, and Félix Guattari. Although it sought to "dis-alienate" patients by rejecting conventional psychiatric treatments and power-relations, institutional psychotherapy refused to be defined simply in terms of what it opposed, and—arguably, unlike the Laingian "anti-psychiatrists"—its practitioners regarded the hospital environment as an active therapeutic and transferential space (Robcis 2021, 1–13). This approach also appears to contradict the principal objective of Basaglia and the Psichiatria Democratica movement, which involved the abolition of psychiatric hospitals and their replacement by the managed reintegration of patients back their communities.

Chapter 3 concludes with a discussion of Nicolas Philibert's 1996 documentary, *Every Little Thing/La Moindre des choses*, a film that is both a portrait of everyday life in the psychiatric community at La Borde, and a homage to Ruspoli's *A Look at Madness*; itself, an important film in the history of documentary that still does not get the critical attention it deserves; much like Ruspoli himself, who "continues to be overlooked, not least because of his experiments aimed at symbolically abolishing the boundaries between filming and filmed" (Graff 2014, 374).

In keeping with the discussion of the aesthetic and political relations between documentary and the critique of psychiatric institutionalisation, Chap. 4 discusses how filmmakers represented alternative therapeutic and pedagogic environments for children and adolescents with complex disruptive behavioural disorders, autism, and other neurodiverse conditions—who would have otherwise spent their lives in state-run psychiatric institutions. The chapter compares two examples within this context: the collaborative films of Fernand Deligny (especially, *The Slightest Gesture/Le Moindre Geste* (1971), and *That Kid, There/Ce gamin, là* (1975)), and Allan King's actuality documentary (or "personal actuality drama", as he termed it), *Warrendale* (1967). Deligny was a radical educationalist (influenced as much by anarchist ideas as by institutional psychotherapy, Jacques Lacan, or Maud Mannoni) who became drawn to the therapeutic and educational potential of documentary filmmaking (or "camering," as he called it). The chapter situates Deligny's career and methods within a broad cultural context and discusses how he wanted to use film to help dissolve the notion of autistic children as "other" and to reduce their alienation and estrangement from the so-called "universe of language." In developing this empathetic anthropology of the image, Deligny deployed film to question the privileging of humanistic concepts of rationality, language, and knowledge from the perspective of so-called marginalised, disabled, "deviant" children and young people.

The chapter also discusses Allan King's film on Warrendale, an alternative and controversial special educational facility outside Toronto, established by social worker and left-wing politician, John Brown, and Dr. Martin Fischer, a child psychologist and play therapist. Under Brown and Fischer's leadership, Warrendale also sought to create a radically empathetic relationship between the young residents and their carers in an environment relatively free from the authoritarian structures and objectifying processes characteristic of other—more typical—therapeutic regimes. The chapter discusses this subject within the context of King's commitment to a democratic, informal, participatory documentary style, an approach influenced by his association with contemporary Beat culture, experimental theatre, and the bohemian communities in Ibiza and London: "King was of a generation that came of age in the 1950s, and his interest in observational cinema was influenced by both psychotherapy and the Living Theatre" (Druick 2010, 4). Interestingly, through the experience of making *Warrendale*, King became a lifelong advocate for new and more radical forms of caring for disturbed and marginalised young people.

During the post-war era, especially during the 1960s and early 1970s, psychiatry also looked to psychedelics (a term first coined in the mid-1950s by the psychiatrist, Humphry Osmond) as a potentially ground-breaking treatment for mental illness. In exploring how documentary film framed the worlds of popular culture and clinical practice at this time, Chap. 5 focuses on Louis van Gasteren's "LSD" documentaries. These films chronicle various psychedelic events and his first-hand experiences during the 1960s—when Amsterdam became the "magic centre"—highlighting Van Gasteren's essayistic documentary style, creative use of archive and found footage, and associative sensibility. In such works—especially, *There is No Plane to Zagreb/Nema Aviona Za Zagreb* (2012)—his enthusiasm for the freedom created by the counter-culture and the vibrant Amsterdam underground scene is tempered both by philosophical preoccupations about the nature of perception and more prosaic concerns about the consequences of psychedelic excess. One of the most interesting sequences in *There is No Plane to Zagreb*, for example, involves Van Gasteren visiting and interviewing Timothy Leary at Millbrook in 1967, followed by his meeting with the guru Meher Baba. The chapter also discusses Van Gasteren's *Now Do You Get It Why I'm Crying?/Begrijpt U Nu Waarom Ik Huil?* (1969), a documentary that directly confronts the experiences of traumatised war survivors and their families in the Netherlands. Sharing some aesthetic similarities with medical education documentaries of the period, Van Gasteren's initial aim was to attract attention to the controversial LSD-assisted psychotherapeutic techniques of the Dutch psychiatrist, Jan Bastiaans (which he had initially intended to include in *There is No Plane to Zagreb*). However, it is the treatment of one of his patients—Jan [Joop] Telling—that emerges as the principal subject of the film, connecting its ostensibly educational and humanitarian theme with Van Gasteren's own traumatic wartime experiences.

As a product of its time, of course, that form of psychedelic-assisted psychiatry—like the work of the Philadelphia Association, or institutional psychotherapy, Psichiatria Democratica, Warrendale, or Deligny—sought an elusive treatment programme or therapeutic environment capable of unlocking or solving the mystery of "madness" once and for all. In this sense, these films convey something of the utopian, idealistic spirit of those times. In contemporary society, of course, the discourse of mental illness seems more complex and postmodern, permeating so many aspects of civil society and the mass media, circulating in a world in which stress, anxiety, depression, grief, trauma, and most forms of neurodiversity are increasingly regarded as typical human conditions often requiring "emotional management" and "resilience skills" rather than psychopharmacological intervention. Yet, perhaps, we should remain wary of some present-day assumptions, and bear in mind that many of the films discussed in this book demonstrate that documentaries dealing specifically with mental illness and its treatments benefit from being available to a variety of artistic influences and experimental possibilities, that the relationship between form and content is integral rather than incidental to the success of any encounter between a filmmaker and the "politics of madness".

The alternative to this approach—and the one which is increasingly commonplace in contemporary Western broadcast media—espouses a formulaic documentary practice and presumes the objective reality and humanitarian integrity of its representations, and in so doing becomes an inadvertent mechanism for re-marginalising and silencing those individuals and communities that comprise its ostensible subject matter. In other words, the problem remains today—as it did for filmmakers back in the

1960s and 1970s—that in front of the camera, the psychiatric subject can all too readily become an object, and the language and structures of any given documentary style risks simply "re-alienating" certain people from the rest of the world, reinforcing the assumption that there are some out there who are mad ("them"), and others observing them who are not ("us"). Or, put another way: are filmmakers and their audiences still akin to the residents of nineteenth century Montevideo, who—according to one of Eduardo Galeano's vignettes: "spent their Sundays on a favourite outing: an excursion to the jail and the insane asylum [...] Contemplating prisoners and lunatics, the visitors felt certifiably free and sane" (Galeano 2018, 58)?

References

Bandosz, B. 2021. Framing and Staging Madness in the Ethico-Aesthetic Paradigm: How Witold Gombrowicz's *Operetka* Expresses Nicolas Philibert's *La moindre des choses*. *Deleuze and Guattari Studies* 15 (3): 411–431.

Daney, S. 2022. *The Cinema House and the World: The Cahiers du Cinéma Years, 1962–1981*, intro. A. S. Hamrah, trans. C. Pichini. Boston: Semiotext(e)/MIT.

Druick, Z. 2010. *Allan King's A Married Couple*. Toronto: University of Toronto Press.

Emerson, H.A. 2021. Reframing Madness with Avant-Garde Film: Lina Mangiacapre's Feminist Collaboration at the Asylum. *The Italianist* 41 (2): 323–337. https://doi.org/10.1080/02614340.2021.1967645.

Evans, B. 2024. The Origins of Film, Psychology and the Neurosciences. *History of the Human Sciences* 37 (2): 12–40. https://doi.org/10.1177/09526951241244979.

Foot, J. 2015. *The Man Who Closed the Asylums: Franco Basaglia and the Revolution in Mental Health Care*. London: Verso.

Forgacs, D. 2014. *Italy's Margins: Social Exclusion and Nation Formation Since 1861*. Cambridge: Cambridge University Press.

Fuller, S. 2012. Samuel Fuller: Survivor: Interview with Tom Ryan [1980]. In *Samuel Fuller: Interviews*, ed. G. Peary. Jackson, MS: University Mississippi Press.

Galeano, E. 2018. *Hunter of Stories*, trans. M. Fried. London: Constable.

Graff, S. 2014. *Le cinéma-vérité: Films et controverses*. Rennes: Presses Universitaires de Rennes. https://doi.org/10.4000/books.pur.76200.

Grimshaw, A., and A. Ravetz. 2009. *Observational Cinema: Anthropology, Film, and the Exploration of Social Life*. Bloomington, IN: Indiana University Press.

Joice, K. 2022. Using Film in the History of Psychiatry. In *Sources in the History of Psychiatry: From 1800 to the Present*, ed. C. Millard and J. Wallis, 215–235. London: Routledge.

Kahana, J. 2008. *Intelligence Work: The Politics of American Documentary.* New York: Columbia University Press.

Marlon, M. 2022. *Camering: Fernand Deligny on Cinema and The Image.* Leiden: Leiden University Press.

McElhaney, J. 2009. *Albert Maysles.* Champaign, IL: University Illinois Press.

O'Sullivan, S. 2017. The Rise of the Feature Documentary—Fact or Fiction? In *DVD, Blu-ray and Beyond,* ed. J. Wroot and A. Willis, 135–157. Cham: Palgrave Macmillan.

Robcis, C. 2021. *Disalienation: Politics, Philosophy, and Radical Psychiatry in Postwar France.* Chicago, IL: University of Chicago Press.

Snelson, T. 2021. From *In Two Minds* to MIND: The Circulation of 'Antipsychiatry' in British Film and Television During the Long 1960s. *History of the Human Sciences* 34 (5): 53–81.

Sontag. S. 1988. Artaud [An Essay]. In *Antonin Artaud: Selected Writings,* ed. S. Sontag. xvii–lix. Berkeley, CA: University of California Press.

Stastny, P. 1998. From Exploitation to Self-Reflection: Representing Persons with Psychiatric Disabilities in Documentary Film. *Literature and Medicine* 17 (1): 68–90.

Vallejo, A. 2020. The Rise of Documentary Festivals: A Historical Approach. In *Documentary Film Festivals,* Framing Film Festivals, ed. A. Vallejo and E. Winton, vol. 1, 77–100. Cham: Palgrave Macmillan.

Witt, C. 2022. The Space of Care: Fernand Deligny, Renaud Victor and the Making of *Ce gamin, là* (1975). *French Screen Studies* 22 (1): 23–43.

CHAPTER 2

Self and Others

Abstract This chapter examines documentary films concerning the radical therapies and persona of R.D. Laing—one of the most well-known and controversial figures of post-war psychiatry, and someone who has remained present in the popular imagination. Laing's celebrity status and the range of his writings and frequent media appearances, as well as his association with "anti-psychiatry" and the counter-culture, made him an attractive subject for documentary filmmakers, and the chapter critically evaluates the documentaries made by Canadian filmmaker, Peter Robinson, in the early 1970s, as well as other films that attempted to capture the essence of the Laingian experience, before concluding with a discussion of Luke Fowler's work, including *All Divided Selves.*

Keywords R.D. Laing • *Asylum* (Film) • Anti-psychiatry • Observational documentary • Schizophrenia • Luke Fowler

On 5th November 1972, R. D. Laing set off for the USA, having agreed to complete a coast-to-coast tour of public talks, lectures, media interviews, workshops, and meetings with friends. The London he left behind that day was cold, damp, hungover, and teetering on the brink of economic recession. Laing's own outlook was also somewhat gloomy: he had new financial worries, and other issues in his personal and professional life

D. O'Rawe, *Documentary Film and Radical Psychiatry*, https://doi.org/10.1007/978-3-031-74231-6_2

were becoming increasingly problematic. Earlier that year, Félix Guattari had predicted "the œuvre of Laing [will] find in the future an even larger readership", citing in support of his claim the fact that "an anti-establishment movement of urbanists, known as CRAAAK [Cirque Rurbain d'Animation, d'Action, d'Agitation Koultourelle] has used [Laing's] poem on childhood from *Knots* as an epigraph of its manifesto": Laing perhaps welcomed the prediction more than another endorsement (1996, 38). Throughout the 1970s, he would try various ways to reinvent—or "rebrand"—himself: out went Laing the firebrand intellectual of the so-called "anti-psychiatry" movement and in came Laing the celebrant of creativity, re-birthing, and Eastern mysticism; but as one of his biographers puts it: "the public didn't welcome Laing's metamorphosis and continued to think of him as the 'old' Laing, or else not at all" (Burston 1998, 124). Although still a celebrity—as the advance ticket sales for his American engagements demonstrated—he was, *pace* Guattari and CRAAAK, in danger of becoming, like the counter-cultural epoch that had expediated his apotheosis, an anachronism: a cultural relic rather than a serious social critic.

Throughout the long 1960s, the medium of film was an essential platform for promoting Laing's work and public image. At one end of the scale, as Michael Staub (2011, 119) speculates, "cult films like […] Bergman's *Persona* (1966) and […] Philippe de Broca's *King of Hearts* (1966) were (each in its own way) reflections and further popularizations of [Laing's] ideas about the socially manufactured nature of madness", while at another David Mercer's collaborations with Ken Loach on *In Two Minds* (1967) and *Family Life* (1971) generated considerable political—and aesthetic—debate (Snelson 2021; Hill 2019, 47–50, 84–89). *Knots*, that aforementioned 1970 book of ludic verse, also inspired both the experimental *Reading Film from Knots by R.D. Laing* (David Lamelas, 1970), and a feature-length film adaptation of Edward Petherbridge's stage play version of the poems (1975).[1] While both of these films play very fast and loose with the distinction between truth and fantasy, this chapter focusses largely on Laing's relationship with documentary filmmaking in a more conventional sense, and on a group of films primarily produced less to dramatize the Laingian project than to observe and preserve its reality, or at least something of that reality.

A HOUSE DIVIDED

Peter Robinson's *Asylum* (1972) portrays communal life in one of the post-Kingsley Hall households (in London's Archway district) established in the early 1970s by Laing and other members of the Philadelphia Association. Robinson found the experience of filmmaking in this alternative therapeutic community challenging but also personally transformative, and although he had initially intended the film to be shot in a rigorously observational mode, he soon embraced its participatory and baroque potential. Born in Canada, Robinson's career began in theatre management, but by the 1960s he was enjoying some success as a producer on documentaries, including Francis Thompson and Alexander Hammid's Academy award-winning multi-screen short, *To Be Alive!* (1964), which premiered at the 1965 World Fair in New York; and as the director of a notable American short, *Susan After the Sugar Harvest* (1971) (Vogel 1974, 138). After reading *The Divided Self* and *The Politics of Experience*, Robinson contacted Laing with a proposal to make a series of television documentaries about the Kingsley Hall community, *State of Mind*, in which Laing would be interviewed, and Sean Connery would provide commentary (Robinson 1970a, 1970c). When that project fell through (although, Laing made various attempts to revive it—albeit in different forms, and at one point involving the BBC and Allan King), both agreed to push ahead with the production of a less ambitious documentary (Robinson 1970b).[2] Several filmed interviews with Laing duly followed before it was agreed that Robinson and a two-person crew would shoot a feature-length observational documentary while living in one of the Philadelphia Association houses. In the early spring of 1971, Robinson, Richard [Dick] Adams (camera and editor), and William [Bill] Steele (sound engineer) resided for six weeks with over a dozen people in a house on Duncombe Road—or rather two houses knocked into one (Smith and Young 1972, 58–59).

While Laing disliked the term "anti-psychiatry"—popularized by David Cooper in 1962 when he was setting up Villa 21 (a pioneering experimental hospital ward in Shenley Hospital, Hertfordshire)—Laing's work similarly challenged the assumption that psychiatric patients were necessarily devoid of authentic agency, or that they were unreachable and incapable of meaningful communication and social interaction. In rejecting the normative medical model of mental illness, Laing had initially turned to psychoanalysis and the emerging psychotherapeutic approaches promoted at the time by figures such as Donald Winnicott, Charles Rycroft, Marion Milner, and John Bowlby at the Tavistock Clinic in London, as well as philosophical paradigms derived from existentialism (especially, Karl Jaspers and Jean-Paul Sartre), and social anthropology (Gregory Bateson and Margaret Mead). At the Tavistock (where his training as a psychoanalyst began in 1956), Laing also conducted important research with Aaron Esterson, and their subsequent co-authored study, *Sanity, Madness, and the Family* (1964), examined schizophrenia through the lens of social phenomenology rather than neurobiological determinism. As a young psychiatrist in the early 1950s, Laing had found himself questioning the efficacy of conventional psychiatric diagnoses, the increasingly routine nature of referrals for electroconvulsive therapy (ECT), insulin-coma treatments and the widespread prescription of anti-psychotic medication (Laing 1985, 95–119). A series of appointments in psychiatric departments at Gartnavel Mental Hospital, and then Glasgow General, had done little to change his generally low opinion of clinical psychiatry.

Focussing instead on the patient as a human being rather than a patient-object afflicted by some pathologically classifiable disease, Laing argued that whatever else "madness" was, it wasn't madness. Rather, it was a particular state of mind and mode of expression, one that responded to imaginative engagement, empathetic listening, and the fact of another person or people "being present": put simply, it was less a mental disorder than a different way of envisaging reality and relating to others. For Laing, the aim of psychiatric care should not be to subject someone to *a treatment* but rather to accompany them on their personal voyage through memories, traumas, dreams, identities, desires, grief, despair, faith, and whatever else was there to be explored; and if there was a therapeutic guidebook or manual for this relationship, Laing contended, it was to be found in the therapist's own sensitivity to the intricate textures of lived experience, and the examples of literature, art, music, and mystical writings, not in the *DSM* or some weighty tome on psychiatric medicine. Laing liked to stress the close etymological relations between the word "therapist" and the ancient Greek word, *therápōn*, which also translates as "attendant" or "companion" rather than simply "healer": "a therapist is someone who pays attention ... who isn't imbued with the ideal of *doing things to* but whose concern is *to let be*", as he remarks during *R.D. Laing in the USA* (Robinson, 1972) (Fig. 2.1).

Inevitably, Laing has been popularly over-identified with the Sixties and an image of himself as one of the counter-culture's leading lights, more

Fig. 2.1 R.D. Laing taking questions at a press conference in 1972. (*R.D. Laing in the USA*, 1973, Peter Robinson)

prophet than physician, wild-eyed shaman than pioneering mental health-care reformer. Thomas Szasz (no friend of existential-phenomenology or left-wing thinking) even went so far as to describe Laing as "a medical-psychiatric conman, a typically modern charlatan 'soul doctor' and master self-dramatiser" (2009, 103). While many aspects of Laing's thought and lifestyle certainly coincided with the iconoclastic *zeitgeist* of the times, and that—as Peter Sedgewick wryly commented—his "political pronounce-ments [were] emotionally radical rather than theoretically articulate" (1971, 28), nevertheless, his contribution to the development of more enlightened approaches to understanding and treating mental illness is considerable, and has remained influential within the fields of social and psychoanalytical psychiatry (Nelson 1972, 226; Itten 2015, 122–32). Even in his last book, *Wisdom, Madness, and Folly: The Making of a Psychiatrist 1927–1957* (1985), Laing was still correcting prevailing misperceptions about his views:

> I never idealized mental suffering, or romanticised despair, dissolution, tor-ture, or terror. I have never said that parents or families or society "cause" mental illness, genetically or environmentally. I have never denied the exis-tence of patterns of mind and conduct that are excruciating. I have never called myself an anti-psychiatrist and have disclaimed the term when my friend and colleague, Dr. David Cooper, introduced it. However, I agree with the anti-psychiatric thesis that by and large psychiatry functions to exclude and repress those elements society wants excluded and repressed. (Laing 1985, 8)

If Laing's occasional appearances in *Asylum* seem merely "inserted" or contrived, it may be because Robinson was wary of making a film that would be inadvertently complicit in contributing to a caricature "R.D. Laing." For the most part, the film's narrative focus remains fixed on the group, and represents figures like Leon Redler, Paul Zeal, and even Michael Yocum, as taking up the torch originally lit at Kingsley Hall.

In keeping with the ethos of the Philadelphia Association, the Archway community aspired to have, as Laing put it, "no staff, no patients, no locked doors, no psychiatric treatment to stop or change states of mind" (Laing 1985, ix). However, as Robinson's *Asylum* shows, there was a discernible organisational structure and some of the residents had defined roles within that structure. Yocum, for example, a "community therapist," was responsible for maintaining some basic house rules and ensuring all the residents contributed to the rent, as well as facilitating—albeit loosely and democratically—ad hoc house meetings to discuss problematic behaviour or conflict between residents. Although Redler and Zeal feature in the film at times as "visiting therapists," there were no Philadelphia Association therapists living in the house during the production of *Asylum*; the residents were all in psychotherapy, but those appointments were arranged separately and not necessarily with anyone connected to Laing, Redler and the Association. In an important sense, the house was just a place where a group of people lived communally, an asylum in the loosest sense of the word.

Laing was travelling in Ceylon (Sri Lanka) and India throughout 1971–1972, and although he appears in several inserted sequences, these are for the most part edited from interviews Robinson had filmed shortly prior to the production proper; and their function in the film is informative, opportunities for Laing to explain what the community is trying to achieve. In another sequence, Laing is filmed sitting silently and attentively amongst a group of residents. The film's prologue, for example, includes footage of Laing in a spacious front room, sitting in an armchair, explaining the origins of the Kingsley Hall community and the importance of adopting non-judgemental and non-interventionist relationships with the other residents. The film then cuts to a panning shot of a skyline of terrace rooftops, travelling along a row of dilapidated—and in some cases, boarded-up—houses on Duncombe Road, before the camera frames a postal worker delivering mail to the house, and a close shot of the number on the front door, "43". The opening of the film pointedly establishes the community as residing on the social margins of the city—in this case, a run-down street in a part of North London designated for redevelopment.

Among the residents who feature in this film (and others), David Bell is perhaps the most memorable, or as the filmmaker and visual artist, Luke Fowler put it: "one of Kingsley Hall's most poetic and visionary residents" (Fowler n.d.). A middle-aged former scientist, he often communicates by scribbling gnomic messages and graffiti, or by speaking in a surreal idiolect (in which Leon Redler, for example, is "the Red Lion", Julia is the "Yellow Rose", and the community itself is referred to as the "happy canny loonies", etc.); and the metaphorical scope of his monologues extends from Pre-Roman Britons ("the *Iceni*") to medieval Zen masters. Initially, unhappy about the presence of the film crew, he became more amenable to them as time passed. Other residents involved include: Julia, a young woman who at times regresses into an extremely helpless, infantile state; Francis Gillett, formerly one of the original Kingsley Hall residents (like David Bell), who mischievously performs for the camera with an exaggerated, antic walk; Jamie, a man in his early twenties from a wealthy rural background; Wendy Galson, another former resident of Kingsley Hall (who subsequently became a psychotherapist); Mary, who is referred to in the 2015 DVD audio commentary as "Sister Mary Simon"; Richard, a working-class Londoner; Paula, a young English woman; Astrid, a Norwegian artist and musician; and Lee, a psychiatrist from Long Island who had "opted out" of mainstream clinical practice to spend time living in a Philadelphia Association community, and who states that he is finding the experience of sharing a house with David extremely difficult—to which David retorts: "People who live in glass houses shouldn't throw stones."

Observing how the others in the house respond to David's disruptive behaviour is dramatically integral to the narrative shape of *Asylum*, but there are other significant threads woven into its content: for example, how the residents (including David—and especially, Mary and Francis) care for Julia; how therapists like Redler and Zeal integrate democratically into the community; and the arrival of various visitors or callers to the house (especially, Jamie's cheque-book waving father, who blithely suggests that a secretly arranged blind date might speed-up his son's "recovery"), or the gauche American medical student (who arrives one Sunday in the hope of using the house as a case-study for his graduate thesis). While one contemporary critic of *Asylum* praised it as "not another audio-visual aid for explanation of another theory of psychology; rather it disturbs normal film rhetoric," it was still—if not quite an "explanation" or exposition—an introduction for many of its first audiences to a practical application of Laing's theories, in which such incidents justify the broader work of the Philadelphia Association, and illustrate its concept of "therapy" (Silverstein 1973, 8).

It is unlikely that the Association would have agreed to the film's production, or the residents given their consent to be filmed (and for it to be released and distributed at all), had its ostensible aim not been to show how living together in this ramshackle communal accommodation can prove to be part of a genuinely therapeutic experience, as opposed to virtual incarceration within the institutionalised mental healthcare regime. While the film adheres to a dramatic structure, the varied and informal quality of its assemblage of sequences also reflects the culture of benign anarchy that exists within the house. That said, the role of Robinson himself in a number of these sequences raises questions about whether such "directorial" participation contributes to, or detracts from, the film's documentary integrity. In one sense, the—sometimes very visible—involvement of Robinson and his production crew in the everyday life of this community is unremarkable: it is an "open house" of sorts in which residents are free to come and go, and—within certain limits—behave however they want. It is also a busy and confined environment and the line between observation and participation constantly dissolves, and while residents like David, Francis, and Astrid are at times clearly performing for the camera, Robinson is careful to keep that reflexive dimension in the final cut: after all, he also performs for the camera. In addition to sequences that include Robinson being part of social situations in the house (or being observed observing), there are two scenes in which he is filmed conversing "privately" with individual residents: firstly, with Jamie; and at the end of the film, with David. In both cases, Robinson adopts a loose conversational style that reflects something of the spirit of Laing's approach to communicating with people who are experiencing psychosis and complex emotional problems and is designed to further blur the line between outsider and insider, filmmaker and therapist. While Robinson seems at worst naively avuncular in encouraging Jamie to be open about what he "really wants," his conversation with David is perhaps more problematic in this context.

If *Asylum* is constructed around a core dramatic event, it is the culmination of the conflict between David and several other residents, a conflict

that tests the therapeutic validity of the entire project and remains unresolved during and after the house meeting that has been convened by
Redler and Yocum. As if to counter this ambiguous outcome, the film's
closing sequence features Robinson appearing to succeed in maintaining a
lucid conversation with a clearly tranquillised David, who mentions details
about his career in scientific research and close relationships. Has Robinson
included this scene to ensure that the film represents David more fully, or
to show how the filmmaker himself—as a supportive presence or *therapist*—can successfully communicate with David on a personal level? If the
latter is the case, are the filmmakers not guilty of exaggerating their integration into the community, elevating themselves and their documentary
motives above those of the other visitors—who the film tends to depict as
muddled intruders, voyeurs, and outsiders? Perhaps, if Robinson had
really wanted to be true to the alternative vision and culture of the
Philadelphia Association, instead of closing the film with his conversation
with David, he might have concluded it with some interviews and footage
from the discussion that took place six months later when he screened a
rough cut of the film to the Archway community (Fig. 2.2).

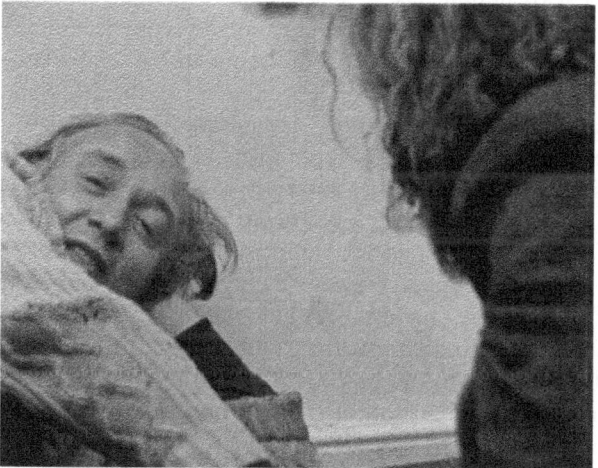

Fig. 2.2 David Bell and Leon Redler at the post-Kingsley Hall house on
Duncombe Road. (*Asylum*, 1972, Peter Robinson)

AMERICAN FRIENDS

Robinson's involvement with Laing lasted for several years, and despite various projects failing to materialise, it was by no means an unproductive relationship for either party. In addition to *Asylum* (which premiered in New York and then London's Collegiate Theatre on 7th October, 1972), Robinson directed and produced two short "interview" documentaries using footage gleaned mainly from his initial meetings with Laing, *Breathing and Running* (1971), and *Psychiatry and Violence* (1971).[3] Robinson and his small production crew also accompanied Laing on his one-month tour across US university campuses (5th November—8th December), returning with nearly forty hours of film, and twice that in audio recording.[4] The resultant short, *R.D. Laing in the USA*, was doubtless edited with an eye to conveying something of Laing's hectic schedule, as well as the intellectual content of his arguments. Unlike *Asylum*, however, *R.D. Laing in the USA* adopts a more rigorously "fly-on-the-wall" observational aesthetic reminiscent of the journalistic Direct Cinema style still in vogue at that time, and something that may be an indication of Robinson's hopes of enticing a US television broadcaster or distributor.

The tour schedule involved "thirty-two talks across the States in thirty-five days," with filming taking place at its beginning and latter stages. *R.D. Laing in the USA* opens with a handheld sequence following Laing as he makes his way through LAX, having just disembarked from yet another plane (Laing 1994, 167). The film cuts to the UC Berkeley main campus, and a series of "vox pop" interviews with several of the event organisers and students, one of whom refers to Laing as "the Mick Jagger of the psychiatry set"; another interviewee—himself an avowed "anti-psychiatrist"—makes a scathing reference to Napa (State Hospital), the large psychiatric hospital located approximately thirty-five miles from Berkeley, a remark that also conveniently highlights the anti-establishment nature of this milieu, one in which Laing seems generally regarded—as another interviewee puts it—as the "most revolutionary figure … since Freud". The action then cuts to a large, packed auditorium where Laing—framed on the stage in an authoritative low angle medium long shot—is recounting a recent case-history to his rapt audience. The film continues in this compilation-reportage format, with no voice-over, inter-titles, or expository context: a medical student challenges Laing (with an insult rather than an argument) only to be rebuffed by Laing's characteristic combination of pugnacity and panache; before the film shows him responding thoughtfully to another individual's post-lecture question. Two sequences tend to interrupt the Direct Cinema tempo: the first begins with Laing playing the piano in a large drawing room before engaging in good-humoured movement and breathing exercises with Alan Watts and some of his circle (including Gertrude Enelow, the author of *Body Dynamics: The Zen and Zest of Self-Development*, 1960); and another in which he and Jutta Werner meet with the Manhattan-based psychoanalyst, Elizabeth Fehr, who demonstrates her approach to "Rebirthing" or "Natal" therapy. These sequences do present the more relaxed and intellectually inquisitive aspects of Laing's personality, as well as situating his own approaches within the broad spectrum of experimental and alternative therapies popular at that time, especially in parts of the USA (Fig. 2.3).

Laing had been interested in the debilitating psychological (and physical) effects of medicalised childbirth practices since his days at the Tavistock (both Bowlby and Winnicott published on this subject), and he saw parallels of violence between modern psychiatric and obstetric medicine; and in many of his own patients, believed he had identified a correlation between traumatic childbirth experiences and adult mental illness. Meanwhile, he was so impressed by Fehr's work that after she visited London in 1973, he

Fig. 2.3 R.D. Laing relaxing with Alan Watts and some friends. (*R.D. Laing in the USA*, 1973, Peter Robinson)

soon began supervising "rebirthing" workshops at the Zeals' house in Maida Vale: "In its most typical [...] form the rebirthee would have to struggle free of something like a six-person rugby scrum [and Laing] usually suggested that bodily emotional catharsis was the most important benefit of the experience [...] but catharsis was not the whole story; rebirthing echoed world-wide initiation ceremonies by invoking the mythological symbolism of death and rebirth" (Edgar and Williams 2021, 251–252). One such workshop was filmed by a Swedish crew and was included in a 1977 documentary on the Philadelphia Association, *The Philadelphia Network/Philadelphia-nätverket* (Oddvar [Bob] Foss).[5] Not only was rebirthing a logical extension of traditional regression therapies, but its symbolic aspects distanced Laing further from the fearsome "anti-psychiatrist" caricature by emphasizing instead his interest in non-Western religions, meditation, yoga, and psychedelics. He may also have hoped that his impassioned denunciations of the "brutality" associated with modern childbirth practices would help to validate his work in the eyes of otherwise sceptical feminists, like Juliet Mitchell or Elaine Showalter, for example, whose respective critiques exposed contradictions (and potentially fatal ironies) at the heart of the Laingian project and its philosophical foundations (Mitchell 1975, 285–292; Showalter 1985, 197–220). More broadly, Lisa Appignanesi has argued that the "anti-psychiatrists" typified the libertarian naivety of the 1960s: "[having] paid little attention to the gender-specificity of their patients' problems [...] their descriptions of the lives of women unwittingly brought women's very specific plight into dramatic view [and] their patients [...] seemed to cry out both for explicitly gendered consideration and for liberation" (Appignanesi 2009, 368). Maggie Tonkin has suggested, however, in a critical reappraisal of Laing's relationship to feminism: "The major feminist criticism of Laing – that he was inattentive to gender – holds true for much of his published work, but [...] late in his career Laing embraced contemporaneous feminist ideas and [...] became more attentive to the phenomenology of women's lives, especially the experience of childbirth" (Tonkin 2019, 250).

Fehr's rebirthing techniques, along with those of the Philadelphia Association, and the publication of works such as Frédérick Leboyer's influential *Birth Without Violence* (1974), inspired the New Zealand actor, family therapist, and natural childbirth campaigner, Helen Brew, to contact Laing about the possibility of involving him in the production of a television documentary exposing the harm caused by current childbirth procedures and maternity care (Brew 1977). Brew may also have been aware of Mike Csaky's 1976 British independent documentary, *How Does It Feel?*, in which Laing is filmed with two women assisting his second wife, Jutta Werner, with the home birth of their third child, Max. The subsequent documentary, *Birth with Dr. R.D. Laing* (1978) was directed by Sam Pillsbury, who had just left the New Zealand National Film Unit and was trying to establish himself as an independent filmmaker, and was included in the "Foundations of Life" series for TVNZ 1. The film adheres to a loosely dialectical structure, with its narrative alternating between: accounts by different women describing the litany of humiliations, surgical interventions, and medications that characterised their experiences giving birth; Laing's reflections on "the horror" of these modern childbirth procedures and the benefits of giving birth naturally; graphic footage of "brutal" clinical births with technocratic doctors and nurses, steel instruments and screaming new-born babies; and homebirths characterised by a much more holistic bonding experience for mothers and their babies. According to Adrian Laing, the film "which showed a new-born baby in extreme physical distress being circumcised without an anaesthetic, left [his father] in tears every time he saw it' (Laing 1994, 190). Certainly, there can be no doubting the sincerity of Laing's denunciation of the traumatising role played by mid-wives, gynaecologists, and clinical technicians in modern childbirth and his conviction that this gruesome *dispositif* be replaced by more natural forms of maternity care and support, as he states in the film: "Instead of a primal scream, we might even have a first sigh, it's a time of coming together or of communion, forming the first ties of love and affection [...] the precious beginnings of lifelong bonds of love and affection ... the shattering of these bonds is the precondition of insanity in later life".

Unlike Robinson, Brew and Pillsbury were working within a more rigid broadcast documentary format, with Laing very much featuring as their film's presiding advocate-presenter. Nevertheless, *Birth with Dr. R.D. Laing* provoked no small amount of controversy, collected Feltex and Melbourne Film Festival awards for best documentary, and aspects of its *mise en scène* remain noteworthy (Brew 1978, 45–51; Kuttna 1978, 117; Laing 1994, 190–91). Throughout, for example, Laing's voice-over seems to hover above the film's starkly contrasting representations of clinical and natural childbirth procedures: the former shown as a scene of trauma and chaos (hand-held framing, screaming babies, the brutally functional application of various obstetric instruments and technologies), while the latter enjoys more inclusive framing and shot structures, Laing featuring in person rather than voice-over, a soundtrack of peaceful silence or harmonious, soothing flute music, and tentative rather than assertive close shots. The contributions from mothers recounting their experiences provide first-hand testimonies that support the film's wider argument. However, while the uneven balancing of observational and participatory methods found in Robinson's *Asylum*, for example, can allow for a degree of ambiguity that reflects—even if inadvertently—a reality about both the virtues and the limitations of the Laingian project, *Birth with R.D. Laing*, for all its laudable humanitarianism, perhaps too readily becomes a polemical exposé, and in a context where the relationship between the medium and the message is never simple, too often seems more a vehicle for Laing's charismatic persona than an advocatory documentary demanding urgent social and medical reform.

Did You Used to Be R.D. Laing?

Laing remained the subject of various television programmes and interviews throughout the 1980s and 1990s. Just prior to his involvement in the production of *Birth with Dr. R.D. Laing*, for example, he had featured in an episode from a thirteen-part Canadian Broadcasting Corporation (CBC) series, "Cities," produced and directed by the London-born filmmaker, John McGreevy. Based around celebrities visiting their favourite city—for example, *Mai Zetterling's Stockholm* (1979) and *John Huston's Dublin* (1980), etc.—McGreevy invited Laing to return to Glasgow. In *R.D. Laing's Glasgow* (1978), Laing retraces his childhood stomping ground, surveys the post-industrial cityscape, admires the civic treasures, tell anecdotes and converses with other notable Glaswegians (including Jimmy Reid (the trade-unionist), Jack Glass (fire-brand preacher), as well as a memorable encounter with the poet, Hugh MacDiarmid). Laing comes across in this film as the consummate raconteur, fondly musing about his hometown and its history. Regardless of financial or other motives, returning to Glasgow to make this otherwise trivial travelogue also "encouraged Laing to (re)imagine his home city and to delve deep in his memories of childhood, [...] that had as much to do with forgetting as remembering, and that was made up of fragments of memories drawn together through his position in an adult world" (McGeachan 2013, 270). The production of *R.D. Laing's Glasgow* involved Laing working again with Charles Stewart, who had previously been the cinematographer on *How Does it Feel?* (part of Roger Graef's BBC/PBS series "The Space between Words"), as well as *Family Life* and *Family* (1972). The experience of writing the screenplay may well have provided him with an added incentive to begin work on what would become *Wisdom, Madness, and Folly*; interestingly, the original title of Laing's draft for *R.D. Laing's Glasgow* was *Glasgow Past and Present: A Personal Memoir* (Laing 1976). Like many a romantic libertarian before him, Laing's turn to autobiographical writing at this stage in his life suggests a puritan, as well as psychoanalytical, motive.

Before his death in August 1989, Laing was still to be seen occasionally being interviewed on chat shows and radio programmes (although, by this stage he was increasingly suffering from the effects of alcoholism). Thomas (Tom) Shandel and Kirk Tougas' documentary, *Did You Used to Be R.D. Laing?* (1987), is one of the better-known film portraits of him in his later years. Primarily produced by TV Ontario, it was made in association with Channel 4, although only broadcast in the UK in October 1989, shortly after Laing's death. Shandel was a mainstream documentary filmmaker and Tougas' background was in experimental film and visual arts, and they had already worked together on a two-part critique of Canada's national health insurance system, *Bitter Medicine* (1983, CBC). Tougas' contribution to their collaborations was mainly as a cinematographer, and it is interesting to note how *Did You Used to Be R.D. Laing?* combines their different backgrounds and aesthetic priorities as it attempts to capture something of the elusive complexity of Laing's persona, as well as the sometimes startling simplicity of his ideas, as he says at one point in the film: "the way we treat one another is the therapy".

The background image to the film's opening titles is a multi-perspective/illusionist oil-painted facial portrait of Laing, which then reappears in more fragmented form at end of the film (to the melancholy sound of Laing's deft piano rendition of "Danny Boy"). The film then cuts directly to Laing, seated on a stage, entertaining an audience with his "Didn't You Used to be R.D. Laing?" anecdote, before a longer sequence in which he is filmed in dialogue with the Canadian psychotherapist (and one of his former PA trainees), Andrew Feldmár (whose wife, the artist, Meredith Feldmár, painted the Laing portrait that features in the film). While *Did You Used to Be R.D. Laing?* presents a largely affectionate version of Laing, showing him recounting various case-histories to audiences, and then—more intimately—in conversation with some individuals who are dealing with their own issues, it too soon panders to the Laing caricature, blurring the distinction between eminent psychotherapist and after-dinner speaker (or even stand-up comic). This problem is also due to Laing's characteristic performance style, giving the impression of someone now condemned to a life spent impersonating himself, an impression strengthened rather than offset by the sequences involving his now mawkish reflections on his upbringing and the consolation of music.

By the 1990s, Laing's radical ideas about existential psychotherapy and his many valid criticisms of clinical psychiatry and perceptions of mental illness increasingly disappeared from documentary treatments about his life and work, or became enveloped in some essentially reactionary, anti-intellectual version of "the Sixties". On the one hand, a film like *Eros, Love & Lies* (1990, Mark Elliott), for example, merely combines footage of Laing dutifully lecturing, reciting poetry, and occasionally reflecting on some general aspect of his approach to life, while *Just Another Sinner: The Life and Times of R.D. Laing* (1994, Eleanor Yule)—commissioned for the BBC's "Ex-S" series—comprises a largely *ad hominem* (re)presentation of Laing's shortcomings as a husband, father, and professional colleague, "supported" by interview extracts and a compilation of archive footage from various sources. Admittedly, since the 1980s—and noticeably in the UK context—much contemporary documentary film has been pressurised into superficial journalistic and biographical formats by the new economies of broadcast media distribution. As opposed to the essay film or more experimental productions, this situation means that any commercially commissioned documentary aiming to reach a large audience cannot—by its very nature—do justice to the complexity and subjectivity of Laing's attempts to encounter mental illness on its own terms. Instead, filmmakers find themselves pandering to the kind of mass audience which, to paraphrase one of Laing's touchstone figures, Carl Jung, finds it easier to judge than to think. Within this context, Luke Fowler's art works on Laing, radical psychiatry, and the long 1960s serve as a necessary and imaginative corrective to this tendency.

BEYOND DOCUMENTARY

Like Laing, Fowler is a Glaswegian, and the city has often been integral to his art and broader cultural concerns. While not a documentary filmmaker in any ordinary sense, his films and installations interrogate the formal relations between perception and representation, biography and portraiture, archive and original, sound and image. His work can evoke a distinctly modernist film aesthetic in both its eschewal of some formulaic, prefabricated narrative, and in its associative rather than illustrative montage techniques: "I see my films as a continuation of my examination and

interrogation of documentary as a form [...] I'm critiquing these domi-
nant forms of representation and how they calcify into what we call documentary" (Balsom 2023). Fowler's asynchronous, and carefully textured
soundscapes, which can comprise fragments of archive recordings as well
as his own electroacoustic and other experimental musical forms, are also
crucial to this process of disrupting and reconfiguring institutionalised
modes of documentary expression.

Three of Fowler's works are related to Laing and his *milieu*, particularly
during the period of his involvement with the Philadelphia Association
from the mid-1960s to the early 1970s.[6] There are various reasons why
Fowler has repeatedly returned to explore the liminal terrain between the
real and mythical "R.D. Laings". Firstly, Glasgow is a key point of reference for Fowler, who relates to Laing's deep connection to the city, its
politics and distinctive psychogeography. Secondly, there are more personal or autobiographical motivations: when Fowler's father experienced
mental illness, he soon found himself entangled in a highly bureaucratised
and pharmacologically-orientated health service that did little if anything
to help him; and Fowler also credits his mother—a sociologist and community activist—in shaping his political attitude to the relationship
between mental illness and social class. Thirdly, while Fowler's work often
focusses on dissident or counter-cultural figures, Laing stands out for him
both as a social radical and as a writer and "performer," as someone who
placed the generosity of art, imagination, and the creative impulse at the
centre of his therapeutic methods. Finally, while Fowler is by no means
simply nostalgic for a new Laingian revolution or naïve to the limitations
of its practices, his work consistently rejects utilitarian concepts of normal-
ity that pathologize defiance, difference, and eccentricity, and that pro-
hibit serious discussion about the fundamental role of society in the
construction of mental illness. Related to this point is the fact that his
work often registers an interest in a specific "*group*, a community—in this
case the mentally ill," and as Martin Herbert suggests, the "parallel
between the micro-communities of his films and the micro-communities
he himself is part of" (Herbert 2012).

In 2001, Fowler produced *What You See Is Where You're At*, a 24-minute
collage film that pays homage both to Laing's essentially compassionate
and socially committed approach to mental illness while also invoking that
approach as a counterpoint to—and critique of—the widespread pharma-
ceuticalization of mental healthcare in contemporary Western society. The
film includes sequences from Robinson's documentaries, several of which

are those featuring David Bell, who was also filmed at Laing's rebirthing workshop in Foss's *Philadelphia Network* (and is then interviewed some years later for *Just Another Sinner*). Fowler is similarly drawn to the story of Bell, and his 2006 installation, *The Nine Monads of David Bell*, further explores the social and emotional dynamics in the Philadelphia Association by situating Bell's dreams, surrealistically tangential use of language, and the trinity of alter-egos Bell refers to in his conversations and writings ("he", "she", and "boy") within an exhibition context. Some of the recordings, documents, and artefacts included in *The Nine Monads of David Bell* were provided by Redler, who had collected them during the thirty-year period he spent as Bell's therapist, friend, and "archivist." Ultimately, the range of elements that comprise the installation—including its 50-minute sound composition, actors filmed enacting Bell's dreams (as he had described them to Redler), texts and "manuscripts" (including old newspapers Bell used as writing paper and which now possess a curiously palimpsestic quality), and Michael Yocum's photographs (which had originally been included in *Philadelphia Network*)—do not simply constitute a *history* of David Bell's conscious, sub-conscious, social, and intimate experiences, they capture something of the nearly ineffable complexity and vulnerability of any life.

In 2011, Fowler returned to Laing in his widely acclaimed, *All Divided Selves*. With a running time of 93 minutes, it is significantly longer than *What You See Is Where You're At*; and his longest film to date, although duration is integral to its expressive structure. It is a formally complex work that in addition to an array of archive and (re)found footage featuring Laing (in everything from chat-shows to newsreel to serious documentaries), it also includes examples of Fowler's own abstract, often poetic, Super-8 and 16 mm footage of nature and changing seasons, the city and its quotidian shapes and sounds. The film's intricate mosaic of moments, images, gestures are frequently drawn from Laing's television interviews with figures like Joan Bakewell or Gay Byrne, and high-profile psychiatrists, such as Morris Carstairs, Desmond Kelly, or Anthony Clare, but they also feature other figures from Laing's world: Aaron Esterson appears, as does Thomas Szasz, and David Cooper, for example. However, instead of these "cited" fragments—which are always both familiar and strange, random and motivated—finding an alternative coherence or congregating around some new, previously undiscovered "R.D. Laing", if anything they maintain the film's essentially anti-biographical quality, maintaining an unbridgeable gap between the

"R.D. Laing" we think we know, and the reality of whoever once was—and still is—R.D. Laing. This unsettling aesthetic manoeuvre immediately generates questions about images and what they signify (*All Divided Selves* seems also to draw on variations of the Kuleshov effect in some of its montage combinations), as well as different image systems and how they "capture" a figure like Laing.

Fowler's work is not only an experimental or abstract take on the complex life and times of R.D. Laing: if anything, it is primarily interested in images of Laing, in how—and why—these images have been framed and edited, circulated and appropriated by modern forms of documentary film and media communication because, as George Steiner famously remarked in 1971: "It is not the literal past that rules us, save, possibly, in a biological sense. It is images of the past."[7]

NOTES

1. *Family Life* (released in the USA as *Wednesday's Child*) was a feature film remake of *In Two Minds*, the 1967 television play written by David Mercer for the BBC's "The Wednesday Play" series. In 1973, Petherbridge had directed and performed in his stage adaptation of *Knots* with the Actors' Company, before collaborating with David Munro on its screen adaptation. The resultant film, directed by Munro, and produced by Simon Perry—also titled *Knots*—premiered during Critics' Week at Cannes in May 1975, and was broadcast on BBC2's "2nd House 2nd Run" series in August of that year. Laing (along with David Cooper) was involved as a consultant in Loach's film, and he also makes a brief cameo appearances as a member of the audience in Munro's *Knots*.

2. According to Hannah Proctor, Robinson had also been "a student of [Peter] Sedgwick's in the late 1960s", which might further account for his interest in political psychiatry, and Laing (2016, 38). Allan King had been involved in the production of Peter Davis' *Anatomy of Violence* (1967), a documentary on the Congress on the Dialectics of Liberation, (which Laing had been crucial in organising through his involvement in the Institute of Phenomenological Studies). According to Davis: "A Canadian company, Allan King Associates, had a studio in London [...] and through them I arranged to film the two-week event, held at the Roundhouse in Chalk Farm, for airing on Channel 13" (Davis 2021).

3. Robinson is also credited as the director of a 1974 educational film featuring Laing and the American psychoanalyst, Harold F. Searles, in which they demonstrate their respective therapeutic approaches through talking—alternately—to a young woman with a psychosomatic condition, *Approaches: Dr.*

Harold Searles and Dr. R.D. Laing (video, col., 43 min.). The film was shot during Laing's 1973 mini-tour of Canada and was produced by a Toronto PR company (Software Productions). It was subsequently distributed privately by Robinson's New York-based production company (Laing 1994, 177). At the time of writing, a shaky version was available to view on YouTube: https://www.youtube.com/watch?v=rB7ow9Rh6Xo

4. In its current form, *R.D. Laing in the USA* has a running time of twenty-three minutes, although the R.D. Laing Collection at Glasgow University currently holds "37.5 hours of film, 82 hours of audio" recorded by Robinson and his crew during this tour (Chapman 2019): http://www.gla.ac.uk/myglasgow/archivespecialcollections/discover/specialcollectionsa-z/rdlaingcollection/#MSLaingAdd1.

5. Foss's 16 mm documentary on the work of the Philadelphia Association was shot in the early 1970s, with Hans Åke Gabrielsson. It was produced by the Swedish Film Institute (Svenska Filminstitutet). Michael Yocum features in the film, which also includes the original montage of his b&w photographs from Archway as he explains his decision to move to another "quieter" PA house. The film includes interviews with PA people like Francis Huxley, Leon Redler, Peter Mezan, Hugh Crawford, and the yoga teachers, Arthur, and Janet Balaskas. *Philadelphia Network* is currently available to view online at the Svenska Filminstitutet website: https://www.filmarkivet.se/movies/philadelphia-network/

6. *Bogman Palmjaguar* (2008) might also be included in this list, given Leon Redler's role in bringing its eponymous subject (a reclusive environmentalist) and his legal case to Fowler's attention.

7. A version of this quotation (taken from Steiner's *In Bluebeard's Castle: Some Notes Towards the Redefinition of Culture*, 1971) was used by Chris Marker (as the epigraph to *The Last Bolshevik/ Le Tombeau d'Alexandre* (1992)), who is another important artistic influence on Fowler's work.

References

Appignanesi, L. 2009. *Mad, Bad and Sad: A History of Women and the Mind Doctors from 1800 to the Present*. London: Virago.

Balsom, E. 2023. Interview: Luke Fowler. *Film Comment*. 27 February. https://www.filmcomment.com/blog/interview-luke-fowler-being-in-a-place-a-portrait-of-margaret-tait-berlinale-2023/.

Brew, H. 1977. *Letter* [to R.D. Laing]. 10 January. R. D. Laing Collection, L237/6. University of Glasgow.

———. 1978. The Making of a Parent. In *Early Childhood in New Zealand*, ed. B. O'Rourke and J. Clough, 39–52. Auckland: Heinemann Educational.

Burston, D. 1998. *The Wing of Madness: The Life and Work of R. D. Laing* (Rev. ed.). Cambridge, MA: Harvard University Press.

Chapman, A.R.D. 2019. *Laing in the USA, 1972—And His Message to the Smartphone Obsessed 21st Century*. University of Glasgow Library Blog: Archives and Special Collections [guest blog post], 18 November. https://universityofglasgowlibrary.wordpress.com/2019/11/08/r-d-laing-in-the-usa-1972-and-his-message-to-the-smartphone-obsessed-21st-century/.

Davis, P. 2021. *Out-Takes*. Villon Films. https://villonfilms.ca/stories/out-takes-2021

Edgar, B., and P. Williams. 2021. 'American Healing': Primal Therapy, Rebirthing, and Cathartic Encounters in 1970s London (and Beyond). *Journal of Transatlantic Studies* 19: 238–260. https://doi.org/10.1057/s42738-021-00072-3.

Fowler, L. n.d. *Luke Fowler*. https://www.luke-fowler.com/

Guattari, F. 1996. The Divided Laing. In *The Guattari Reader*, ed. G. Genosko, 37–41. Oxford: Blackwell.

Herbert, M. 2012. Undivided Attention: The Art of Luke Fowler. *Artform* 51 (2) https://www.artforum.com/features/undvided-attention-the-art-of-luke-fowler-205937/.

Hill, J. 2019. *Ken Loach: The Politics of Film and Television*. London: Bloomsbury.

Itten, T. 2015. Psychotherapeutic Compassion in the Tradition of R.D. Laing. In *The Legacy of R.D. Laing: An Appraisal of his Contemporary Relevance*, ed. M. Guy Thompson, 122–132. London: Routledge.

Kuttna, M. 1978. Edinburgh—The Way Out Film Festival. *Self & Society* 6 (4): 115–118. https://doi.org/10.1080/03060497.1978.11086718.

Laing, A.C. 1994. *R. D. Laing: A Life*. London: Harper Collins.

Laing, R.D. 1976. Manuscript [R.D. Laing: Draft entitled *Glasgow: Past and Present...*], 29 November. R. D. Laing Collection, MS Laing A505. University of Glasgow.

———. 1985. *Wisdom, Madness, and Folly: The Making of a Psychiatrist: 1927–57*. London: Macmillan.

Laing, R.D., and A. Esterson. 1964. *Sanity, Madness, and the Family*. London: Tavistock.

McGeachan, C. 2013. (Re)remembering and Narrating the Childhood City of R.D. Laing. *Cultural Geographies* 20 (3): 269–284. https://doi.org/10.1177/1474474012462532.

Mitchell, J. 1975. *Psychoanalysis and Feminism: Freud, Reich, Laing and Women*. New York: Vintage.

Nelson, B. 1972. Afterword: A Medium with a Message. In *Laing and Anti-Psychiatry*, ed. R. Boyers and R. Orrill, 297–301. Harmondsworth: Penguin.

Proctor, H. 2016. Lost Minds: Sedgwick, Laing, and the Politics of Mental Illness. *Radical Philosophy* 197: 36–48. https://www.radicalphilosophyarchive.com/article/lost-minds/.

Robinson, P. 1970a. Letter [to Sean Connery], 15 October. R.D. Laing Collection, L238/99. University of Glasgow.

———. 1970b. Letter [to R.D. Laing], 6 November. R. D. Laing Collection, L238/100. University of Glasgow.

———. 1970c. Letter [to R.D. Laing], 15 December. R.D. Laing Collection, L238/98. University of Glasgow.

Sedgewick, P. 1971. R. D. Laing: Self, Symptom and Society. *Salmagundi* 16: 5–37. https://www.jstor.org/stable/40546633.

Showalter, E. 1985. *The Female Malady: Women, Madness, and English Culture, 1830–1980*. New York: Pantheon.

Silverstein, N. 1973. Two R.D. Laing Movies: *Wednesday's Child* [*Family Life*] and *Asylum*. *Film Quarterly* 26 (4): 2–9. https://doi.org/10.2307/1211481.

Smith, H., and T. Young. 1972. Review of *Asylum*, *Village Voice*, 28 September, 58–59.

Snelson, T. 2021. From *In Two Minds* to *MIND*: The Circulation of 'Anti-Psychiatry' in British Film and Television During the Long 1960s. *History of the Human Sciences* 34 (5): 53–81. https://doi.org/10.1177/09526951211023334.

Staub, M.E. 2011. *Madness Is Civilization: When the Diagnosis Was Social, 1948–1980*. Chicago: University of Chicago Press.

Szasz, T. 2009. *Anti-Psychiatry: Quackery Squared*. Syracuse: Syracuse University Press.

Tonkin, M. 2019. R.D. Laing, Feminism and the Politics of Birth and Re-birth. *Australian Feminist Studies* 34 (100): 248–262. https://doi.org/10.1080/08164649.2019.1570817.

Vogel, A. 1974. *Film as a Subversive Art*. New York: Weidenfeld & Nicolson.

CHAPTER 3

(De)Institutionalisation

Abstract This chapter takes a comparative look at how various documentary filmmakers engaged with both the Basaglian "revolution" in Italy, which campaigned for the abolition of psychiatric hospitals and the managed reintegration of patients back into their communities, and the work of the institutional psychotherapy movement in France. In particular, the chapter discusses *San Clemente*—a film that offers important insights into the scale of Franco Basaglia's task, and Depardon's own troubled relationship with the documentary and photographic representation of psychiatric patients and environments. In relation to institutional psychotherapy, the chapter analyses Mario Ruspoli's *A Look at Madness* (1962), and its relationship to figures such as François Tosquelles at the psychiatric hospital at Saint-Alban, Lozère. The chapter concludes with a discussion of the Clinic at La Borde, and the films made about it, notably Nicolas Philibert's *Every Little Thing* (1996).

Keywords Political documentary • Franco Basaglia • *San Clemente* (Film) • Institutional psychotherapy • *A Look at Madness* (Film) • François Tosquelles • La Borde Clinic

D. O'Rawe, *Documentary Film and Radical Psychiatry*, https://doi.org/10.1007/978-3-031-74231-6_3

In February 1977, Artkino (a Turin-based film distribution co-operative) agreed to distribute *Asylum* in Italy, with Giulio Einaudi contracted to publish an accompanying book comprising an Italian translation of the film's "screenplay" and an introduction written by Franca Ongaro Basaglia, who was married to Franco Basaglia. Artkino duly informed Laing of their plans: "The publishing house and Franca Basaglia, and we of course, intend to present the film (original copy with subtitles) and the book together in Milan towards the end of March. Members of Psichiatria Democratica, journalists specialised in psychiatric information and film critics will be invited" (Artkino 1977). In response, Laing promptly instructed his solicitors to threaten Artkino and Robinson with legal action if the event went ahead, demanding the right to inspect any such publication prior to its distribution.[1] There are some interesting aspects to this incident, not the least of which being Laing's behaviour. He was always eager to see his work receive credible international attention, and he had hitherto valued Robinson's documentaries as a constructive contribution in that regard. By the mid-1970s, however, Laing had effectively parted company with the Philadelphia Association (or rather, it from him). Perhaps, he felt that *Asylum* was no longer representative of his work and should be archived rather than revived, or that he was annoyed (with some justification) at being an afterthought to a project in which his initial support and collaboration—authorship, even—had been instrumental. It is also possible that he was not particularly well-disposed towards the prospect of the Basaglias commenting further on his theories and "prefacing" Robinson's film. Franca Ongaro had already variously translated into Italian key works by Maxwell Jones, Erving Goffman, and Gregorio Bermann, and her interview with Laing had been published in 1975. The Basaglias had visited Kingsley Hall in the late 1960s, and in their *La maggioranza deviante* (1971), they had concluded that the Laingian version of "the therapeutic community" was politically ineffectual, that it encouraged "the illusion [...] that you can somehow 'leave the game,' and attempt to create a non-organised organisation which is outside the world of 'power' and its institutions" (Foot 2015a, 120).

TEARING DOWN THE ASYLUM

Franco Basaglia began his career as an academic psychiatrist influenced by the post-war revival of existentialist thought, and hermeneutical phenomenology. His world view was also shaped by the complicated social history of Italian fascism, a history that included his own experience of political imprisonment for six months at the end of the war. Fascism, war, and post-war economic hardship in Italy conspired to perpetuate deeply-held prejudices against mental illness, and such attitudes were reflected in the atrocious conditions in which psychiatric patients were still being kept in hospitals and asylums throughout the country. For Basaglia, the abolition of these institutions was also part of "a more generalised critique of power, social control and the production of marginality, deviance and difference in capitalist societies, of which the *manicomio* (mental hospital) came to be treated as just one example" (Forgacs 2014, 211). The Basaglias were never without allies in their struggle for fundamental changes to Italy's mental health care regime in the 1960s and 1970s, but the founding of Psichiatria Democratica in 1973 was due in no small part to their combined efforts, as was the approval of the Law 180 ("Basaglia's Law") in 1978. With their years of activism now vindicated by this new legislative provision, the Basaglias and others pressurised for effective implementation of its directives, and for political assurances that the transition from a culture of psychiatric hospitalisation to community-based mental healthcare structures would be carefully managed and adequately resourced. Unfortunately, winning the peace would prove as difficult as winning the war: Basaglia died in 1980, and "the struggle against total institutions would go on for another twenty years *despite* the law" (Foot 2015a, 383).

In early 1977, Raymond Depardon travelled to Trieste on a photojournalistic assignment covering a story about the San Giovanni Psychiatric Hospital, which was being closed and transformed into a therapeutic community, with no new patients being admitted and existing patients being gradually reintegrated into society. The developments in Trieste exemplified the radical agenda being set by the Psichiatria Democratica movement, and its implications reverberated beyond Italy. According to Depardon, Basaglia encouraged him to support the campaign by visiting other *manicomi*, and producing a body of photographic work that would help to document and further publicise the appalling conditions in these institutions: "You'll photograph patients here who you won't see anywhere else, but it's exactly the same in France and America. The psychiatric hospital made them that way; now it's too late, there's nothing else I can do for them [...] Take your photographs, otherwise people won't believe us" (Depardon 2014, npg). For the next four years, Depardon periodically visited various *manicomi* (principally, in and around Turin, Arezzo, Naples, and Venice), photographing everyday life in the asylums and hospital psychiatric wards. It would prove a productive experience: in addition to the feature-length documentary, *San Clemente*, shot in February 1980 with Sophie Ristelhueber; in 1984, he published a series of photographs in an exhibition catalogue (with an accompanying essay by Bernard Cuau), followed by his 2014 photography book, *Manicomio: Secluded Madness*, and various contact sheets provided the images for his contribution to a French television short film series, *Contacts* (1989), in which he ruminates on the relations between voyeurism and aestheticism, intrusion and projection (Depardon 1984).

Depardon and Ristelhueber were of course not the first documentary filmmakers to explore the Basaglian struggle to close the asylums, although *San Clemente* is notable in terms of its subdued "after the revolution" context and especially austere *mise en scène*. By the mid-1970s, Basaglia's radical approach to mental health care had attracted considerable international as well as national interest, especially after the publication of *L'istituzione negata/The Institution Denied* in 1968, and there was growing popular support for dismantling the asylum system in Italy (Basaglia and Ongara Basaglia 2018). The progressive policies introduced by Basaglia and his "*équipe*" at Gorizia in the 1960s had readily reflected the counter-cultural *zeitgeist*, and the media interest their work attracted served to present—albeit simplistically—Basaglia as a fearless, anti-authoritarian liberator of the marginalised and oppressed. Sergio Zavoli's television documentary, *The Gardens of Abel/I giardini di Abele* (1969), which features Basaglia and documents events at Gorizia, is perhaps the best-known example from this era. Broadcast in January 1969, it "[put] the Gorizia experiment on the national map [...] and has become a key part of the way Gorizia is narrated and remembered" (Foot 2015a, 220–21). Although the film emphasizes the contrasting realities of closed and open institutions, and the relations between social class and mental health, while also giving a voice to the patients themselves, it is also a film embroidered with "a Zavolian social and quasi-religious reading of what was going on", in which "onto [its] Basaglian traits, Zavoli added the 'poetry' that came from the combination of the images and the words being spoken, both in the voiceover and by the interviewees [...] He used and manipulated and commented upon the patient's words to make his own points about the lack of value in the 'outside world'" (Foot 2015a, 223).

Zavoli also included footage from other Italian "asylum documentaries" in *The Gardens of Abel*—"none [of which] was credited in the version for TV"—and these sources included: Riccardo Napolitano's *1904, n.36.* (1967); and both Michele Gandin's shorts: *The Open Door /La porta aperta* (1968), and *The Excluded/Gli esclusi* (1969) (Foot 2014, 604). Interestingly, these films also borrow sequences and images from elsewhere, including the Giorgio Osbat archive collection and its iconic scenes (staged by Basaglia) of patients pulling down some of the fences at Gorizia; and a sequence involving a patient being forced into a straitjacket (which features in both *1904, n.36* and *The Open Door*).[2] A musical composition by Egisto Macchi was used in all three of these short documentary films. In the mid-1960s, Macchi began improvising and experimenting with "found sound" and *musique concrète,* and he incorporates actual noise and random voices from the hospital into his musical score. The films also include literary references from both the sixteenth century poet, Tasso (his "letters from the madhouse" are quoted in *1904, n.36*) and more contemporary authors (an important line of text for the Basaglias from Primo Levi's *If This is a Man/Se questo è un uomo* (1947) features in *The Open Door*), and still photographs from the psychiatric hospitals at Gorizia, and at Nocera Superiore. *The Excluded,* for example, makes ample use of Luciano d'Alessandro's photographs from Nocera (and he is listed as the camera operator in the credits for *1904, n.36*). D'Alessandro was invited to take photographs of the appalling conditions at the Nocera asylum by its psychiatric director, Sergio Piro, who also provides commentary for the film. D'Alessandro first published some of his photographs in *Photography Italiana* in 1967, before then using the images as the basis for *The Excluded* (its original release title, *Gli esclusi,* was also the Italian release title of a recent popular Hollywood film on a similar subject, *A Child Is Waiting* (1963, John Cassavetes)). Given Franca Ongaro's direct involvement (as screenwriter) in *The Open Door,* it not surprising that it emerges as the least "modernist" of the three, and while they are all shaped around a shared commitment to bring about urgent, radical change by using arresting images and soundscapes that emphasize the brutal, custodial— rather than remedial—nature of these institutions, *The Open Door* gives the clearest insight into how the Basaglias conceived of documentary film and photography as entirely instrumental to their cause.

The Finish filmmaker, Pirkko Peltonen, had been similarly inspired by *L'istituzione negata,* and after reading it while travelling through Italy, she managed to secure co-production funding from Finland's national broadcaster (Yleisradio) and the Italian public broadcasting service (RAI) for a documentary short on Gorizia, *The Fable of the Serpent/La favola del serpent* (1968). Peltonen had a background in radical student theatre and—like her Italian husband, the journalist and future socialist politician, Carlo Rognoni—she was committed to left-wing political causes at that time. Much of her documentary comprises footage from the debates and votes at the assembly in Gorizia, interspersed with long hand-held sequences tracking the asylum's perimeter fences and ramshackle estate (accompanied by some experimental sound-effects), reminiscent of Alain Resnais' *Night and Fog/Nuit et brouillard* (1956). Also including an interview involving Basaglia, *The Fable of the Serpent* is more than just a compilation of archive footage, and Peltonen clearly edited the film with a view to communicating the universal relevance of what she was witnessing. Basaglia also appears in *Are the Poor Mad?/I poveri sono matti?* (Maurizio Rotundi, 1971), which was filmed not in Gorizia or Trieste but in the closed psychiatric hospital of Santa Maria della Pietà in Rome. As its title suggests, and not unlike aspects of *The Gardens of Abel*, it focusses on the nature of the asylum within the context of poverty and wider causes of social alienation. Framing the issue of mental health care in material as well as humanitarian terms was at the heart of the Basaglian project, and documentary film offered a particularly effective way of illustrating this relationship to a mass audience.

The involvement of internationally renowned psychiatrists, political activists, and artists was also an important feature of the Italian deinstitutionalisation campaign. On the eve of the approval of "Law 180", for example, Amedeo Fago directed *What if I Have a Lion That Eats My Heart/Se ho un leone che mi mangia il cuor* (1977). This is a remarkable film that owes much of its archival value to the involvement of Giuliano Scabia, the playwright and experimental theatre director who had been associated with Group 63 and had worked with Carlo Quartucci and Paolo Grassi. In the early 1970s, Scabia became involved with some like-minded avant-gardists (including Basaglia's cousin, Vittorio Basaglia) in creating the iconic *macchina teatrale*, "Marco Cavallo" ("Marco the Horse")—a four-metre-high papier-mâché blue horse on wheels that became—and still is—the mascot of Italy's deinstitutionalisation movement and its struggle to secure improved mental healthcare provision. The film, which again features Basaglia talking directly to camera, centres around a 1977 workshop, "Réseau internazionale di psichiatria", held in Barcola, near Trieste. As a way of marking Basaglia's achievements in Trieste, Scabia's "wandering theatre" exuded a spirit of street carnival and anarchic creativity, and involved figures like Dario Fo, Félix Guattari, and

David Cooper. A constant in these films is Basaglia himself, urgently articulating his analysis of the current situation and what needs to be done.

Another filmmaker worth mentioning in this context is Silvano Agosti,
who edited *Fit to be Untied/Matti da slegare* (1975) and is credited as a
co-director on the film (with Marco Bellocchio, Sandro Petraglia, and
Stefano Rulli), and who also directed *The Flight/Il volo* (1975), a documentary short featuring contributions from the Marxist sociologist, Maria
Grazia Giannichedda, and Cooper. *Fit to be Untied*, which had an initial
running time of well over two hours (and was originally titled, *None or
All/Nessuno o tutti*), is a collective intervention in support of the changes
taking place at the mental hospital at Colorno, in the Emilia-Romagna
region. In keeping with the ethos of deinstitutionalisation, the film combines conventional *vérité*-style interviews with Brechtian agit-prop techniques to simultaneously frame and de-frame the reality of events on the
ground rather than simply "reporting" from within the psychiatric hospital (Forgacs 2014, 243–50). The distinctive and unsettling *engagé* aesthetic of *Fit to be Untied* owes much to Agosti's editing and reflects the
importance of radical left-wing politicians (especially, Mario Tommasini
and the PCI) in spearheading the transformation of mental health structures in that region rather than the psychiatrists: Basaglia had endured a
short, difficult spell working there before he headed to Trieste.

While it is impossible to know whether Depardon and Ristelhueber
knew any of these documentaries, or others on the same subject, in aesthetic and political terms *San Clemente* is a different kind of film to *Fit to
be Untied*, and it is unlikely ever to be described as "Zavolian." The sense
of place and the people in *San Clemente* possess a particularity that dis-
courages interpreting the institution as a metaphor for the outside world.
However, it would be surprising if Depardon had not been familiar with
the Basaglias' co-edited photo-book, *Morire di classe/Death by Social Class*
(1969), and how that book configures relations between Carla Cerati and
Gianni Berengo Gardin's photographs and the accompanying selected
quotations from literature, social theory, radical psychiatry (esp.
Goffman)—at times ironically interspersed with extracts from hospital
policies and regulations (Basaglia and Ongara Basaglia 2008; Foot 2015b).
Morire di classe was not unique in terms of how it created associations
between and across photographic images and text, but it did adopt a creative approach that might have been appealed to Depardon at that time.

By the end of 1970s, he was disillusioned with the world of corporate
photojournalism, and his 1979 book, *Notes*, marked a significant shift in

his visual style from observational or journalistic detachment to a more open, subjective, and autobiographical approach. Depardon's motivation in changing his documentary methods so fundamentally was structural as well as personal: throughout the 1970s, television had consolidated its predominance in the world of media communication, leaving traditional forms of photojournalism and documentary filmmaking struggling to survive in a market where the demand for quality picture magazines was declining rapidly (between 1971–1972, for example, both *Life* and *Look* called it a day, and even the circulation figures for a celebrity-orientated magazine like *Paris Match* more than halved between 1958–1972). In its uncompromising critique of what much photojournalism has become, even Depardon's 1981 documentary, *Reporters*, seems to offer a justification for his decision to take his work in a different direction. While *San Clemente* registers the expressive and ethical implications of that new approach: its subject matter and the act of filming the patients also highlights a tension between the desire to frame and control, and the pursuit of a looser and more tentative documentary style.

CONTACT

Unlike photography, film increasingly enabled Depardon to articulate an experience of reality that was free to follow reactions, promptings, and intuitions in the language of long takes and handheld cinematography, where the framing is careful but not necessarily precise, and more available to coincidence and uncertainty. Throughout *San Clemente*, the soundtrack's uncanny assortment of ambient sounds (especially, radio music), noise (talk, footsteps, squeaking doors) and silence supplements the film's images of fidgeting figures walking aimlessly in circles, pacing up and down the "white" corridors, dancing monotonously, or just sitting in silence, motionless. At key moments in the film, however, both Depardon and Ristelhueber become involved in the action (in the literal sense of this word), especially when individual patients ask them random, unexpected questions or try to take possession of the camera or microphone. From the outset the film acknowledges its availability to the complexities of the relationship between the filmmakers and the patients and staff at the hospital: the pre-title sequence culminates with a doctor or nurse telling the filmmakers not to enter a particular ward, reprimanding them: "Shame on you!"

Although he has tended to align his documentary style with the Direct Cinema tradition rather than *cinéma vérité*, comparisons with Frederick Wiseman's work—especially in relation to their shared interest in the often converging worlds of psychiatric and judicio-legal institutionalisation—are understandable but not necessarily instructive (Marcel 2009, 18–19). Halfway through *San Clemente*, for example, there is a sequence that illustrates some of the distinctive characteristics of Depardon's method. The sequence in question lasts just over four minutes. It is a single hand-held *plan-séquence* comprising both moving and static images. Opening with a shot of a mounted television broadcasting a "live" Catholic mass, the camera tilts down to frame a small, hunched elderly woman standing slightly behind an adjacent doorway, holding a ragdoll in her arm. The sound of the television resonates loudly as the woman stares back into the room, and at nothing. Two nurses pass her and walk through another double-door. She watches them and follows for a couple of steps, stops, and turns back before walking out of the shot as Depardon's camera turns and tilts back upwards at the television again. Continuing its travels, the camera then veers left and enters a small adjoining ward, where another woman can be seen sitting alone on a bed, languidly combing her hair. The camera dollies back, framing in medium shot the woman holding the ragdoll, with the sound of a choir (singing the Sanctus) emanating loudly from the television set. The camera pans left and ventures into a larger recreation area where several women are sitting quietly on chairs before panning right and into a busy office (whereupon Depardon and Ristelhueber are shooed away by one of the nurses). Backed into the sitting area again, there follows a gradual circular panning shot, before the filmmakers are approached by a woman with a broom, who gestures angrily at the camera and shouts, "Stop that!" She forces the broom at the camera lens but withdraws when a nurse appears off-screen, joking that this woman is just "attention-seeking." The camera follows the nurse through another double-door into a men's recreational area, before cutting to the next sequence.

On the one hand, Depardon's preferred *plan-séquence* structure seems to militate against imposing a singular perspective by allowing the camera to happen upon incidental fragments of the real. The spontaneous interaction with patients and their families, as well as the medical staff, suggests compassionate curiosity, openness, and a desire to respect the other and the value of their experience and voice. On the other hand, as David Forgacs has argued: "the film's voyeuristic passages, those in which the patients are merely observed and do not speak, or their voices cannot be heard, tend to present their otherness as a fixed and inexplicable condition" (Forgacs 2014, 243). While Basaglia was supportive of Depardon's work on the *manicomi*, this was not—as the film shows—necessarily the case for everyone involved. Perhaps, *San Clemente* is as much about the problem of filming psychiatric subjects, as it is about the condition of the asylum itself, exploring how its own seemingly "innocent" observational style conspires in concealing the filmmakers' essentially intrusive and voyeuristic motives. It may even be more instructive to consider *San Clemente* as one component in a larger series of related works that would include the *manicomi* photography books and the short film, *Contacts*, in which Depardon himself subsequently ruminates on the morality of photographing mental illness and human suffering. *San Clemente* invokes a fundamental dilemma facing anyone seeking to film or photograph inside the asylum, and this dilemma is not convincingly resolved just because they subsequently acknowledge the possibility of moral negligence on their part (Fig. 3.1).[3]

Fig. 3.1 Preparations for a party at the psychiatric hospital on San Clemente, Venice, Italy. (*San Clemente*, 1982, Raymond Depardon and Sophie Ristelhueber)

HEALING COLLECTIVES

Just as the Basaglias had taken issue with Laing over his withdrawal from the political fray, there were some who felt that the ideology of Psichiatria Democratica was itself predicated on a simplistically oppositional, deterministic concept of society, and the meaning of mental illness within that context. Félix Guattari, for example, while broadly sympathetic to much of what the Basaglias and Laing wanted to accomplish, nevertheless argued for a more complex, nuanced, "rhizomatic" approach to these questions:

> Political causality does not completely govern the causality of madness. It is perhaps, conversely, in an unconscious signifying assemblage that madness dwells, and which predetermines the structural field in which political options, drives, and revolutionary inhibitions are deployed, beside and beyond social and economic determinisms. (Guattari 1996b, 44)[44]

For Guattari, the supposedly rational, technocratic basis of traditional psychiatric treatments and psychoanalytical therapies overlooks the full array of influences and socio-economic investments that are continually shaping and reshaping subjectivity: these treatments and therapies belong to a psycho-political model of control in which the relationship between modernity and schizophrenia, for example, can be less one of an illness in need of a cure than a cure in need of an illness. The task of what Guattari coined "schizoanalysis", then, is to subvert the hegemony of the oedipal paradigm, attending instead to the contradictions of subjectivity, and the endlessly productive, deterritorializing, ineffable workings of desire, or as he and Deleuze memorably elaborated in their *Anti-Oedipus: Capitalism and Schizophrenia* (1972): it involves "learning what a subject's desiring-machines are, how they work, with what syntheses, what bursts of energy in the machines, what constituent misfires, with what flows, what chains, and what becomings in each case"(Deleuze and Guattari 1996, 92).

Guattari's philosophical and therapeutic rejection of Basaglian deinstitutionalisation is also a defence of institutional psychotherapy, an approach that seeks to reinvent or reimagine the psychiatric institution rather than abolish it completely. Originating in the 1930s, this essentially communitarian form of psychiatry came to prominence after the Second World War (especially given that 40,000 mentally ill people had died largely due to a Vichy policy of intentional negligence, or "soft extermination" (Max

Lafont), in France's psychiatric hospitals between 1940–1945), and with the arrival of François Tosquelles to the psychiatric hospital at Saint-Alban, Lozère in 1941 (Von Bueltzingsloewen 2009). Working alongside other progressive psychiatrists like Lucien Bonnafé and Georges Daumézon, Tosquelles implemented an alternative therapeutic model that was holistic, collective, and "multi-disciplinary" (or "pluri-disciplinary"), incorporating into conventional psychiatry ideas and treatments derived from psychoanalysis, psychology, anarcho-syndicalism, Marxist theory, existential phenomenology, but also the visual arts, performance, and creative therapies. Institutional psychotherapy was versatile, improvisational, democratic, and always predicated on the assumption that mental illness was simultaneously personal and structural; and while psychiatric hospitals would continue to exist (offering an *institutional* frame), they should be "non-concentrationary," and integral to—not separated from—wider community and civil society. Institutional psychotherapy sought to "disalienate" patients by rejecting conventional psychiatric treatments and power-relations, and it refused to be defined simply in terms of what it opposed, and—arguably, unlike the "anti-psychiatrists" or Psichiatria Democratica—its practitioners regarded the hospital environment as an active therapeutic and transferential space: "the hospital—its architecture, its activities, its staff, represented [what Tosquelles referred to as] a *collectif soignant*, a 'healing collective'" (Robcis 2021, 40).[5] In Mario Ruspoli, Tosquelles and institutional psychotherapy would find a documentary filmmaker whose expertise and eclectic sensibility seemed ideally suited to the task of filming the life of Saint-Alban.

THE ROAD TO SAINT-ALBAN

Ruspoli's career as a documentary filmmaker began with his involvement in journalism, and especially through his contributions to *Constellation*, a popular digest magazine of the late 1950s and early 1960s. As was often the case during this period, the step from print to broadcast journalism could be a surprisingly small one, and Ruspoli soon found himself producing—and even presenting—current affairs programmes (especially, for Télé-Luxembourg). In terms of developing his own distinctive documentary style, however, he—like Jean Rouch and Chris Marker—was ambivalent about the label, *cinéma vérité*. Initially, he preferred the term *cinéma direct*, which is more closely related to the French and Canadian formulation of Direct Cinema than the North American version championed by figures such as Robert Drew and Richard Leacock. Although the subject of much debate at the time, the boundaries between these approaches can seem indiscernible from a distance, and in one sense they are all products of the same transformations in mass culture and filmmaking technologies: television, and new lightweight, "noiseless" cameras alongside improvements in processing film stock that increasingly reduced the need for heavy lighting equipment (Van Cauwenberge 2013, 189–90; Graff 2014, 275–324). The ability to combine the new KMT Coutant with a portable Nagra tape-recorder, and a lavaliere ("clip-on") microphone enabled filmmakers to walk and talk in synchronicity with the camera.[6] By the time Ruspoli travelled to the Lozère to make his ethnographic documentary about this impoverished, agriculturally underdeveloped region in the south-east of France, his modest crew included: the Canadian cinematographer, Michel Brault; Roger Morillière, who had also been involved in the production of *Chronicle of a Summer/Chronique d'un été* (1961), as had Ruspoli's editor on this occasion, Jean Ravel. Working with these individuals, and this new camera, offered Ruspoli a filmmaking experience less *about* documenting a social reality than getting *inside* that reality to reveal it in a new phenomenological complexity, developing a method that "expands and clarifies Rouch and Edgar Morin's view of the ambivalence of the camera as a self-effacing 'observational tool' and as something which provokes a reaction" (Van Cauwenberge 2013, 194).

Ruspoli would elaborate on his concept of *cinéma direct* in 1962, with both the production of his *Method 1* (a 28-minute "manifesto film" made for Radiodiffusion-Télévision Française (RTF)), and a report he authored for UNESCO, *The Lightweight Synchronized Cinematographic Unit: For a Cinema in the Developing Countries* (Ruspoli 1963). Seeking to embrace the opportunities created by the recent advances in filmmaking technology, he advocated a method that would liberate the documentary image from both the ideology of the picturesque, as well as commonplace didactic or journalistic approaches: "[instead] this cinema [...] demands thought, a perpetual exchange with the screen, and self-criticism even on the part of the audience" (Marcorelles 1973, 148). In keeping with the emerging tenets of *cinéma direct,* Ruspoli wanted to explore the margins of contemporary society by integrating the film crew into communities, and vice-versa, allowing stories and conversations to emerge through informal participation rather than strategic provocation, adopting a perspective on social reality characterised by a measured neutrality rather than conscientious objectivity, by a spirit of openness and curiosity, which also included an ongoing exploration of the forms and possibilities of the medium itself. Ideally, there would be no post-synching or post-production editing of images to a prepared script: the structure and shape of the film would be determined by the voices, gestures, actions and reactions of its participants: as much as possible, it would be *their* film; which is not to suggest that *cinéma direct* was shot in continuity or was averse to découpage: for Ruspoli's *The Earth's Forgotten/Les Inconnus de la Terre* (1961), for example, seven hours of footage was finally edited into a thirty-five-minute film (Bovier 2011, 15).

On completing that film, Ruspoli and this crew began work on *A Look at Madness/Regard sur la folie* (1962)—which focusses on daily life at the psychiatric hospital at Saint-Alban, also situated in the Lozère region. The final cut of the film ran to forty-seven minutes, and its producer, Anatole Dauman, tried to maximise Argos' distribution options by dividing it into two short films; the second of which centred on the annual fête or party at which patients, former patients, families, doctors, nurses, locals, etc. gather in the grounds of the hospital to parade in fancy dress, dance, and play games. Ruspoli's relationship with Dauman became strained during the production of *A Look at Madness*, largely because the latter was concerned about spiralling costs, the substantial creative role Ruspoli had given to the psychiatric team, and potential legal problems associated with filming and identifying individual patients (Graff 2014, 141–42; Dauman and Gerber 1992, 39–40). Titled *La fête prisonnière* or *Les Portes de la raison* (17 min.), this newly created "second film" does possess a certain narrative autonomy but is best regarded as the concluding segment or epilogue to the original rather than as a separate short documentary, and when first broadcast on French television in 1962, both parts of *A Look at Madness* were recombined as a single film (Berton 2011, 9; Graff 2011). Not only do the same people appear prominently in both films, but sequences in the "first" include patients hand-printing a poster for the fête, while an important scene involving a patient making confetti in the workshop only really makes sense when we see that same confetti being thrown around during the fête; similarly, one of the games at the fête involves throwing a ball to knock off a hat worn by a character wearing a papier-mâché mask resembling Tosquelles; or even the final sequence from *La fête prisonnière*, when Brault turns his camera on the audience (static, and in close-up), in dramatic contrast to the long, panoramic shots of Saint-Alban at the opening of *A Look at Madness* (as if consciously concluding the film with a

Fig. 3.2 Tossing balls at "Dr. Tosquelles". (*A Look at Madness/Regard sur la folie*, 1962, Mario Ruspoli)

valedictory shot to "de-establish" any potential self-effacement of camera and crew) (Fig. 3.2).

If the emphasis in the "first" film is placed on the clinical environment and the organization, activities, and meetings taking place in the hospital, the "second" completes that picture by showing how the fête represents the incorporation of a carnivalesque dimension to the therapeutic culture at Saint-Alban, as Ruspoli's inter-title card puts it: "More than a party [...] a place for encounter, for treatment, a way amongst others to reconnect, renew, and restore broken communications." For Michel Foucault, the highly theatrical, performative, and communal nature of such asylum activities reveals the paradox at the heart of psychotherapy itself (i.e. that while its theories may be to all intents and purposes scientific and modern, its practices still rely on pre-modern rituals and traditions to make sense of madness): "And by a strange paradox, by a strange return, we organise for [the patients], around them, with them, a whole parade, with dance and mask, a whole carnival, which is in the strict sense of the term a new feast of fools" (Venable 2021, 60–61; Robcis 2021, 114–115). *Pace* Foucault, what Dauman may have overlooked in his decision to separate *A Look at Madness* into two films is the possibility that—unlike traditional psychiatric hospitals or asylums—everyday life at Saint-Alban indicated a willingness to acknowledge and explore this paradox, and the activities of the patients' co-operative or the Club Paul Balvet, for example, were not "extra-mural" or supplementary recreational events but integral to the therapeutic environment, and organised around collective, democratic procedures.

Ruspoli's sensibility, political sympathies, and documentary methods were certainly congruent with the ethos of institutional psychotherapy, especially in relation to Saint-Alban, where "the medical staff worked to develop a 'politics of madness' anchored in psychoanalysis, anarchism, and surrealism" (Robcis 2021, 47). According to François Pain, who spent most of his career working and filming at La Borde: "Tosquelles was plugged into surrealism [...] He was like a character coming from the theatre [...] I liked the way he spoke about surrealism: something more real than real" (Walker-Billaud 2024). In emphasizing the importance of surrealism to both institutional psychotherapy and *cinéma direct*, Mireille Berton lists various aims and approaches common to both: the shared desire to democratize and rejuvenate their respective practices or "disciplines" (psychiatry and documentary); a commitment to creating an environment in which hierarchies would be subordinate to collective, collaborative endeavour; becoming advocates for attentive listening and giving voice to those individuals and communities undergoing treatment, or being represented; placing especial importance on "speech" and the act of speaking openly, associatively, randomly; and, of course, encouraging and harnessing creative and artistic activity and expression (2011, 62). Interestingly, Berton also describes *A Look at Madness* itself as "un film surréaliste", and just as surrealism left its mark on many of those associated with institutional psychotherapy (most notably, Lacan, Tosquelles, Lucien Bonnafé, and Jean Oury), so too Ruspoli's documentary aesthetic is as much a mosaic of glimpses than an exercise in capturing real events as they unfold in view of the camera.

The opening sequence from *A Look at Madness*, for example, features text by Antonin Artaud, taken from his correspondence with Jacques Rivière from the early 1920s, in which Artaud famously defends his poetry as authentic literary formulations expressed from the depths of severe mental illness. While Artaud had fraught relations with the Surrealist movement, he is invariably associated with it, and especially in relation to his 1938 book of essays, *The Theatre and its Double/Le Théâtre et son Double*. A psychologically unstable individual who suffered throughout his life from severe psychotic episodes and catatonic breakdowns (not to mention harrowing psychiatric interventions), Artaud's preoccupation with his "madness" led him to not only question the authority of rationality, and distinctions between being and performance, experience and representation, but especially "the scandal of a thought separated from life, even when he is given over to the most direct and savage experience that ever made the essence of thought understood as separation, of that impossibility that it asserts against itself as the limit of its infinite power" (Blanchot 2003, 40).[7] At the beginning of the film, the quotations from Artaud's heroically defiant letters to Rivière (chosen by Tosquelles; and his fellow psychiatrists, Roger Gentis and Yves Racine) emphasise the necessity of rejecting normative categories and definitions of reason, madness, art and truth (Berton 2011, 52).

Another pre-credit sequence further re-frames assumptions about how this documentary will approach "madness" and the role of the asylum: a title card outlines the scenario and petitions the audience to approach this subject with an open mind ("Que l'on entende, même dans l'angoisse, ce message du monde de la folie …"); followed by a series of close shots of a male patient (Riquet) who briefly but movingly recounts his life experience, his hardships and loneliness (he also features in the "La fête prisonnière" segment); the film's opening credit sequence then follows before cutting to a series of panoramic shots of the village and milieu of Saint-Alban, with the hospital (a former fortress-turned-sanatorium) clearly visible in the frame. Artaud's words (spoken by Michel Bouquet) accompany Brault's camera as it probes and manoeuvres its way along the corridors and through the wards and beds: "a central collapse of the soul […] a veritable paralysis […] a staggering central fatigue, a kind of grasping fatigue […] A fatigue as old as the world, the sense of having to carry one's body around, a feeling of incredible fragility which becomes a shattering pain" (Artaud 1988, 64–65). No doubt, many in the audience would have also recognised Bouquet as the narrator of Resnais' *Night and Fog*, which evokes another set of histories and "concentrationary" associations.

Although Tosquelles is the figure most readily identified with Saint-Alban in the post-war period, *A Look at Madness* is careful not to become a hagiographic portrait of any individual therapist. In fact, the first extended sequence involving a psychiatrist talking to a patient features Gentis and a woman, "Mme Blanche." In another sequence, a young man

Fig. 3.3   François Tosquelles at a meeting with filmmaker, Dolorès Grassian. (*A Look at Madness/Regard sur la folie*, 1962, Mario Ruspoli)

discusses his condition with another psychiatrist. Shot in a close-up and with most of his face obscured by darkness, he talks about his ongoing struggles with anxiety, and feelings of melancholy. The film then cuts to a shot of a reel-to-reel tape recorder playing back his words to three (and then four) psychiatrists (including Horace Torrubia, and Tosquelles) at a later meeting (Fig. 3.3).

The segment also includes a close shot of two finches in a cage in this office, and towards the end Brault's camera seems to drift towards a window and a patient standing alone, outside. There are various dimensions and expressive layers to this sequence. While fragmentary, it offers a sympathetic representation of someone articulating their loneliness, and other people listening carefully to those words and pauses. In clinical terms, it also depicts an early form of the "Cassette Method" of supervision that Tosquelles would subsequently use extensively when he moved from Saint-Alban to L'Institut Pere Mata in Reus (not long after the production of Ruspoli's film). There is also the presence of a visual metaphor in the sequence and an awareness of how documentary is always an inadequate, fragile form that—like institutional psychotherapy—can only succeed by constantly interrogating its potential and limitations, or as Seàn Cubitt once put it: "Documentary operates by Zeno's paradox, constantly approximating but never seizing a real which flees before it" (Chanan 2007, 56).

Given that *A Look at Madness* was produced in collaboration with the staff (rather than just in consultation with them) and that the anti-hierarchical aspirations of institutional psychotherapy involves extensive collective responsibility and decision-making between staff and patients, the film's most *direct* moments tend to occur during meetings and group discussions, at which times the filmmaking process is afforded a certain invisibility as people appear to forget that the camera and recorder are also in attendance. In one such sequence the issue of how the film itself might be serving to simplify and misrepresent the reality of life at Saint-Alban and institutional psychotherapy becomes a topic of conversation between the psychiatric staff at their weekly Sunday morning meeting. The fact of being filmed also raises the question of their self-consciousness and how this can distort an approach to therapy predicated on the freedom to improvise. Comments made by patients are analysed (for example, that the nurses resemble museum guards) in relation to whether the patients might feel they are being "exhibited" by this film production, and how viewers of the film might misinterpret what is happening at any given moment. *A Look at Madness* may differ in many respects from *Chronicle of a Summer*, but its cinematography is similarly attentive to the significance of the spoken *and* unspoken word, voices of dissent and assent, and certainly some of these discussions are reminiscent of the reflexive qualities associated with Rouch's documentary practice.

Framing La Borde

Although Guattari's concept of schizoanalysis was initially derived from his involvement with Lacan, its evolution was also a direct product of both his relationship with Deleuze, and his lengthy career as a psychotherapist at La Borde Clinic. Established in 1953 by Jean Oury (himself a former student and colleague of Lacan), La Borde was an extension of the hospital at Saint-Alban and was similarly associated with institutional psychotherapy, offering holistic, heterogeneous alternatives to mainstream medical psychiatry in France (Reggio and Novello 2007, 32–45). Although the Groupe de Travail de Psychologic et de Sociologie Institutionnelles was not formally constituted until 1960, and institutional psychotherapy had already been inaugurated in the 1930s by people such as Agnès Masson, Paul Balvet, Henri Ey, and Georges Daumézon, it is chiefly identified with Tosquelles, who had arrived at Saint-Alban carrying Lacan's doctoral thesis (*De la Psychose: Paranoïaque dans ses rapports avec la personnalité* (1932)) amongst his few hurriedly packed possessions. Tosquelles' revolutionary socialist beliefs and political activism remained integral to his approach to psychiatry, and his rejection of a system in which psychotic patients were subjected to hospitalisation and crude combinations of tranquilisation, insulin injections, and electric shocks. His work at Saint-Alban attracted the attention of other left-wing psychiatrists, resistance activists, and artists, including Lucien Bonnafé, Horace Torrubia, Hélène Chaigneau, Jean Ayme, Ginette Michaud, and Frantz Fanon—who completed a residency at Saint-Alban in 1951, and published a paper with Tosquelles in 1954. Saint Alban was also a formative influence on Oury, who similarly envisaged La Borde as an asylum without doors, embodying the collective, democratic ethos of institutional psychotherapy.

Unlike Psichiatria Democratica and the Philadelphia Association, Tosquelles, Oury, and Guattari did not believe in the de-institutionalisation of mental healthcare *tout court*, any more than they were interested in campaigning for gradual reforms within the official structures—*établissement*—of French psychiatry. Viewing alienation as always both psychological and sociological, they refused to recognize disciplinary boundaries, always aiming to create an environment—"setting" or "network"—that was institutional but free from the rigid forms of regulatory constraint and power hierarchies evident in typical psychiatric hospitals. At La Borde—a former chateau surrounded by forty hectares of woodland, meadow, and ponds—there were no uniforms to distinguish staff from patients, with staff regularly allocated duties outside their respective spheres of medical, clerical, or technical expertise (in accordance with the famous weekly grid, or *grille*). Everyone—staff, residents, or visitors—participated in twice-daily meetings, at which they were fully involved in role-playing games and group activities. Like Basaglia and Laing, the institutional psychotherapists were not opposed to psychopharmacological intervention as part of a wider treatment plan, which would also include regular one-to-one psychoanalytical sessions, occupational ergo-therapy and paid manual and administrative work.

"Le club" was also an integral part of the therapeutic programme at La Borde; run primarily by the patients, it was responsible for organising recreational activities, such as concerts, the clinic newsletter (*La Borde Éclair*), parties, and the annual play (performed on 15th August). The diversity of activities taking place at La Borde underpinned a core element of its larger therapeutic objective—namely, the creation of an environment conducive to collective transference or "transversality," as Guattari began calling it in the mid-1960s (Guattari 2009; Goffey 2016, 38–47). In other words, typical hierarchies, distinctions, and boundaries within the clinic were constantly being dismantled or reconfigured to ensure that the object of transference is never simply the individual psychiatrist or therapist but the community, where the flow and circulation of transference is unrestricted and determined by both individual and collective responses, including those of the medical staff. It was this environment that Nicolas Philibert chose to visit in the summer of 1995, ostensibly to make a film based around the preparations and rehearsals for that year's play, *Operetka*, an absurdist social satire by Witold Gombrowicz. First performed in 1969 at Teatro Stabile dell'Aquila, it is also an operetta that was written without an original score, making it an attractive choice for resourceful theatre producers and amateur drama groups ever since (Bandosz 2021).

In many respects, La Borde would seem an ideal subject for Philibert to explore: his films are typically preoccupied with questions of how we connect and communicate meaningfully with one another, and how differences might be overcome by little, unspectacular gestures of kindness, humour, sympathy, and mutual respect. He is also very interested in psychiatric care and relationships between therapists and patients (two of his more recent documentaries, for example, *On the Adamant/Sur l'Adamant* (2023) and *At Averroès & Rosa Parks/Averroès & Rosa Parks* (2024) are parts of a planned triptych of documentaries focussing on mental illness and how it is being treated in Paris, especially through day-centres, community out-patient provision, and home visits). Although Philibert and Depardon arrived at documentary filmmaking from quite different backgrounds, their observational styles—like their shared interest in forms of psychiatric care—are not entirely dissimilar, with Philibert also interested in the practice of everyday life as seen through its institutions (schools, theatres, museums, Radio France, etc.). His films are also typically devoid of voice-over commentary or structured interviews, and are characterised by carefully framed long takes, edited to ensure that nothing jars or distracts the audience; even an occasional cutaway to a close shot of an object or detail, or longer shots involving some feature of the landscape, or just to nothing at all, are silently woven into the film's deceptively simple fabric. Philibert also prefers not to be constrained by an overly detailed script or rigid production plan, envisaging the process of filmmaking as involving the discovery of a film that is already there rather than producing a predetermined version of reality: "I make my documentaries from a position of ignorance and curiosity [...] I don't need a map; I don't need to know the final destination [...] the film is an invitation" (Philibert 2012). While this open approach might even chime with the spirit of institutional psychotherapy's notion of "non-deductive ontology", Philibert holds the view that the only way to get inside the reality of everyday life at La Borde is by staying outside its history, approaching it as a stranger and not under the spell of its personalities or politics: "the less I know, the freer I am" (Philibert 2005).

For its part, La Borde has been the subject of various films, most notably Igor Barrère's *La Borde ou le droit à la folie/La Borde, or the Right to be Mad* (1977), a television documentary that culminates in extensive interviews with Oury and Guattari, and *Min Tanaka à la Borde/Min Tanaka at La Borde* (1986, Joséphine Guattari and François Pain). Barrère was a medical doctor and television journalist (known largely through his work in the 1960s on ORFT's current affairs series, *Cinq Colonnes à la une*) and his documentary on La Borde was inspired by the 1976 publication of a book with the same title, written by two psychotherapists who had worked there for over a decade, Jean-Claude Polack and Danielle Sivadon. Guattari and Pain's short film, on the other hand, explores how resident and visiting avant-garde artists like Tanaka also contribute to the work and culture of La Borde (Polack 2011). Pain had also collaborated with Félix Guattari for a number of years at the clinic, and in addition to producing various film and visual art works inspired by schizoanalysis, he also worked with Polack and Sivadon on a 1989 documentary, *François Tosquelles: The Politics of Madness/François Tosquelles, Une politique de la folie*.[8] Unlike these films, *Every Little Thing* approaches La Borde and institutional psychotherapy more obliquely, taking its bearings from an alternative poetics of filmmaking, one that embraces the notion of the observational documentary as being primarily an expressive form concerned with the possibility of meaning rather than the certainty of its production. By centring on the preparations and performance of the annual play, *Every Little Thing* emerges as less an authoritative critique, exposition, or homage to the form of psychotherapy practised at La Borde than a more tentative exploration of what the language of documentary film can and cannot articulate. This point can be illustrated by looking at a particular segment from mid-way through the film.

After showing the actors rehearsing some complex singing arrangements, the film cuts to a static close-up of a man, sitting on the edge of a
bed, wearing an African tribal mask, which then falls or "slips" to reveal his
face (Michel), and enigmatic smile. After a few silent seconds, the film cuts
(rather than tracks) to a full shot of Michel—still sitting on the bed—
now holding the mask on his lap. The camera lingers again as he shuffles
slightly, appears to start moving but remains where he is. This sequence is
followed by two more static full shots: the first frames another
patient, Claude, sitting alone in a kitchen, staring at the floor, and rubbing
his forehead in an agitated way; the second, a medium close shot of
another man, this time lying on his bed, quietly upset, and gazing for-
lornly into Philibert's camera. There then follows a longer sequence
involving coffee and tea being poured and distributed amongst various
people, at one of the club gatherings. This busy scene comprises more
conventional hand-held, observational cinematography, especially in how
it configures the various facial close-ups as people react to—and interact
with—Sophie as she sketches a portrait of one of the groups. This sequence
is interrupted as the film then cuts to Claude again, this time getting his
beard trimmed. Claude's exchanges with the young member of staff who
has volunteered to be his "barber" are comical as they tease one another,
with Claude complaining, and even pretending to fall asleep at one point.
The segment then cuts back to the art club, as Sophie shows off her sketch
and responds to comments and suggestions before this segment concludes
by returning outside again, as two of the actors are shown testing the
sound effects for the play (produced by gently beating a large sheet of
metal hanging from a tree).

Like other segments in the film, this one begins and ends with scenes of
rehearsal and preparations for the play and is particularly illustrative of
Philibert's documentary style and filmic sensibility. *Every Little Thing* culminates with the performance of *Operetka* and in a curious way the play—
this play—frames the entire film and underwrites its *mise en scène* of flux,
ambiguity, and improvisation. The slightly surreal sequence involving
Michel with the tribal mask emphasises this point—his gestures inviting
the audience to ask itself who is performing to whom? What is behind the
mask? What is real and what is reflected? Who is happy and who is sad,
sick, or well, rational, or not rational? The preponderance of carefully
composed static shots adds to the sense of theatricality and artifice, especially towards the end of this segment after Claude's beard has finally been
trimmed and both men are framed in the reflection of a large mirror, their

identities doubled, duplicated by the same image within an image. Without abandoning a coherent narrative structure or subverting the broad conventions of the observational mode, *Every Little Thing* poses questions at every turn, holds meaning (and judgement) in a state of play by refusing to settle into some conventionally realistic—and therefore, moralistic— homage to the La Borde Clinic, and institutional psychotherapy.

NOTES

1. As things panned out, the screenplay was published by Einaudi in August 1977: *Asylum: Un film su una comunità psichiatrica di R. D. Laing*, edited by Ongara and with its authorship attributed to Robinson.
2. In 2015, the Hamburg-based artist and illustrator, Stefano Ricci, collaborated with Jacopo Quadri (editor/filmmaker), and Giacomo Piermatti (musician), to produce an experimental film, sound composition, and illustrated book based on the collection of Gorizia hospital films held at the Giorgio Osbat Archive. Born in Gorizia, Osbat (1920–1996) was an amateur 16 mm filmmaker who ran the local cine-club. In the mid-1960s, he was invited by Basaglia to film inside the psychiatric hospital. Ricci, Quadri, and Piermatti's multi-media *Here They Are/Eccoli/Les Voilà* includes footage from music therapy sessions (led by Francesco Valentinsig).
3. Depardon's preoccupation with psychiatric processes and their relationship to the French criminal justice system has been the subject of some of his other feature-length documentaries, including *12 jours* (2017), and *Urgences* (1987); which was reviewed by Guattari, who praised the "véritable accès" it gives to the "l'intériorité de la folie et de la dereliction" (Guattari 1988).
4. Towards the end of his review essay, "The Divided Laing", for example, Guattari argues that the "anti-psychiatry of Laing, Cooper, Basaglia and several others […] will either be renewed by a widespread, profound modification of the attitudes and the relations of force in everyday practice, or it will remain what it is by circumstance: a literary phenomenon and, as such, already largely 'recuperated' by the most reformist, indeed the most reactionary, currents which never shrink from making verbal concessions […] Anti-psychiatry lays itself particularly open to the reformists' 'recuperations' because on the doctrinal level it did not divest itself of a personalist and humanist ideology" (1996a, 38). In the closing line of his review of Mary Barnes and Joseph Berke's *Mary Barnes: Two Accounts of a Journey Through Madness* (1971), Guattari pointedly refers to "the reactionary implications of [the Philadelphia Association's] psychoanalytical postulates" (Guattari 1996c, 54).
5. For cogent introductory discussions of institutional psychotherapy, see: Robcis' (2021, 1–13); and Faramelli (2023, 161–168).

6. The iconic KMT Coutant-Mathot Éclair "weighed only 1.5 kilograms but could still carry a 400-ft magazine with ten minutes running time" (Henley 2010, 157–158). This important advance in camera technology soon associated filmmakers like Ruspoli and Rouch with the term "le cinéma léger," and its connotations of "travelling light," or a style of documentary filming that is mobile and fleet of foot. In her important study of this topic, Séverine Graff has argued that typical historiographical and critical assumptions about the extent to which technological innovation contributed to the emergence of *cinéma verité* as an aesthetically coherent documentary school or movement are either exaggerated or erroneous, especially in the French context (Graff 2014, 19–29).
7. There is also a relationship between Artaud and Saint-Alban in that Jean Dubuffet—the innovator of Art Brut—visited the hospital in the late 1940s, and not only "shared the Surrealist fascination with madness [but] became especially aware of the specificity of the hospital setting after paying regular visits to his friend [...] Artaud, who spent the last years of his life in the psychiatric hospital of Rodez" (Robcis 2021, 45).
8. See also, Emmanuelle Guattari's autobiographical *I, Little Asylum* (2015). Interestingly, Nazim Djemaï's, *À peine ombre/Out of the Shadows* (2012) is less concerned with the diversity of activities and therapies at La Borde, and although it features an interview with Oury (who died in 2014), it eschews an idyllic depiction of the clinic and its environs.

References

Artaud, A. 1988. *Antonin Artaud: Selected Writings*, ed. and intro S. Sontag. Berkeley: University of California Press.
Artkino: societa cooperativa di distribuzione cinematografica [Letter to R.D. Laing]. 1977. 8th February. R. D. Laing Collection, B1999/1. University of Glasgow.
Bandosz, B. 2021. Framing and Staging Madness in the Ethico-Aesthetic Paradigm: How Witold Gombrowicz's *Operetka* Expresses Nicolas Philibert's *La moindre des choses. Deleuze and Guattari Studies* 15 (3): 411–431. https://doi.org/10.3366/dlgs.2021.0448
Basaglia, F., and F. Ongara Basaglia. 2018 [1968]. *L'istituzione negata: rapporto da un ospedale psichiatrico* [The Institution Denied: Report from a Psychiatric Hospital]. Milan: Baldini & Castoldi.
———. 2018 [1971]. *La maggioranza deviante: L'ideologia del controllo sociale totale* [The Deviant Majority: The Ideology of Total Social Control]. Milan: Baldini & Castoldi.
———. Eds. 2008 [1969]. *Morire di classe: La condizione manicomiale fotografata da Carla Cerati e Gianni Berengo Gardin* [Death by Social Class: The

Condition of Asylums Photographed by Carla Cerati and Gianni Berengo Gardin]. Trieste: Duemilaeuno Agenzia Sociale.

Berton, M. 2011. *Regard sur la folie*: poétique et politique de la folie et du cinéma. *Décadrages* 18: 47–68.

Blanchot, M. 2003. *The Book to Come*, trans. C. Mandell. Stanford: Stanford University Press.

Bovier, F. 2011. Regards sur 'l'impouvoir': le 'cinéma direct' de Ruspoli, de la terre à l'asile. *Décadrages* 18: 14–13.

Chanan, M. 2007. *Politics of Documentary*. London: BFI.

Dauman, A., and J. Gerber. 1992. *Anatole Dauman: Pictures of a Producer*. London: BFI.

Deleuze, G., and Guattari, F. 1996. The First Positive Task of Schizoanalysis [1972]. In *The Guattari Reader*, ed. G. Genosko, trans. R. Hurley, M. Seem, and H. R. Lane. 77–94. Oxford: Blackwell.

Depardon, R. 1984. *San Clemente, ex. cat.* Paris: Centre national de la photographie.

———. 2014. *Manicomio: Secluded Madness*. Göttingen: Steidl.

Faramelli, A. 2023. Introduction: Why Institutional Analysis, Why Now? *Deleuze and Guattari Studies* 17 (2): 161–168. https://doi.org/10.3366/dlgs.2023.0509.

Foot, J. 2014. Television Documentary, History and Memory: An Analysis of Sergio Zavoli's *The Gardens of Abel. Journal of Modern Italian Studies* 19 (5): 603–624. https://doi.org/10.1080/1354571X.2014.962258.

———. 2015a. *The Man Who Closed the Asylums: Franco Basaglia and the Revolution in Mental Health Care*. London: Verso.

———. 2015b. Photography and Radical Psychiatry in Italy in the 1960s: The Case of the Photobook *Morire di Classe* (1969). *History of Psychiatry* 26 (1): 19–35. https://doi.org/10.1177/0957154X14550136.

Forgacs, D. 2014. *Italy's Margins: Social Exclusion and Nation Formation Since 1861*. Cambridge: Cambridge University Press.

Goffey, A. 2016. Guattari and Transversality: Institutions, Analysis, and Experimentation. *Radical Philosophy* 105: 38–47.

Graff, S. 2011. *Filmographie de Mario Ruspoli. Décadrages* 18: 9–12.

———. 2014. *Le cinéma-vérité: Films et controverses*. Rennes: Presses Universitaires de Rennes. https://doi.org/10.4000/books.pur.76200.

Guattari, E. 2015. *I, Little Asylum*, trans. D.S. Burke and C. Porter. Cambridge, MA: Semiotext(e)/MIT Press.

Guattari, F. 1988. *Urgences*: la folie est dans le champ. *La Monde*, 9 March. http://www.palmeraieetdesert.fr/Urgences_in_the_press.html.

———. 1996a. The Divided Laing [1972]. In *The Guattari Reader*, ed. and trans. G. Genosko. 37–41. Oxford: Blackwell.

———. 1996b. Franco Basaglia: Guerrilla Psychiatrist [1970]. In *The Guattari Reader*, ed. and trans. G. Genosko. 42–45. Oxford: Blackwell.

————. 1996c. Mary Barnes's Trip [1973]. In *The Guattari Reader*, ed. and trans. G. Genosko. 46–54. Oxford: Blackwell.

————. 2009. La Borde: A Clinic Unlike Any Other. In *Chaosophy: Texts and Interviews 1972–1977*, 176–194. Cambridge, MA: Semiotext(e)/MIT Press.

Henley, P. 2010. *The Adventure of the Real: Jean Rouch and the Craft of Ethnographic Cinema*. Chicago: University of Chicago Press.

Marcel, J. 2009. Depardon, Wiseman … La meilleure façon decapter. *24 Images* 143: 18–19.

Marcorelles, L., with N. Rouzet-Albagli. 1973. *Living Cinema: New Directions in Contemporary Film-Making*, trans. I. Quigly. New York: Praeger.

Philibert, N. 2005. You Can Make a Great Film with a Very Tiny Subject [Interview with Geoff Andrew, NFT], 5th February. https://www.bfi.org.uk/news-opinion/news-bfi/interviews/nicolas-philibert-interview

————. 2012. I Have No Idea What My Films Are About, *Guardian*, 28 June. https://www.theguardian.com/film/2012/jun/28/nicolas-philibert-what-my-films-are-about

Polack, J.-C. 2011. Analysis: Between Psycho and Schizo. In *The Guattari Effect*, ed. E. Alliez and A. Goffey, 57–67. London: Continuum.

Reggio, D., and M. Novello. 2007. The Hospital is Ill: An Interview with Jean Oury. *Radical Philosophy* 143 (May/June): 32–45.

Robcis, C. 2021. *Disalienation: Politics, Philosophy, and Radical Psychiatry in Postwar France*. Chicago: University of Chicago Press.

Ruspoli, M. 1963. *The Lightweight Synchronized Cinematographic Unit: For a Cinema in the Developing Countries/Pour un dans les pays en voie de développement: le groupe synchrone cinématographique léger*. Paris: UNESCO.

Van Cauwenberge, G. 2013. Cinéma Vérité: Vertov Revisited. In *The Documentary Film Book*, ed. B. Winston, 189–205. London: BFI.

Venable, H.L. 2021. The Carnival of the Mad: Foucault's Window into the Origin of Psychology. *Foucault Studies* 30: 54–79. https://doi.org/10.22439/fs.vi30.6268.

Von Bueltzingsloewen, I. 2009. *Hécatombe des fous: La famine dans les hôpitaux psychiatriques français sous l'Occupation*. Paris: Flammarion.

Walker-Billaud, M. 2024. What I Learned from Tosquelles: An Interview with François Pain. *Museum of the Moving Image*, 20 June. https://scienceandfilm.org/people/936/mathilde-walker-billaud.

CHAPTER 4

Alternative Pedagogies

Abstract This chapter looks at how documentary filmmakers approached alternative therapeutic and educational environments for children and adolescents with complex disruptive behavioural disorders, autism, and other disabilities. The chapter compares two examples within this context: the collaborative films of Fernand Deligny from the early 1970s, and Allan King's *Warrendale* (1967). For Deligny, the pedagogic potential of filmmaking (or "camering," as he called it) was considerable, especially in helping to dissolve the notion of autistic or neurodiverse children as "other" and reducing the effects of alienation and estrangement through "language." King's film centres on "everyday life" in a controversial special educational facility outside Toronto. *Warrendale* not only observes the relationships between the young residents and their carers, it also frames King's support for new and more radical ways of caring for disturbed and marginalised children and young people.

Keywords Documentary film • Childhood • Autism • Fernand Deligny • Allan King • *Warrendale* (Film)

The 1948 Christmas issue of *Life* magazine carried a feature, "Children of Europe", comprising eleven photographs by David "Chim" Seymour, who had been commissioned by UNICEF to produce a photographic report on the plight of European children orphaned, displaced, maimed, and impoverished by the Second World War. Although it is impossible to arrive at a precise figure, contemporary commentators and humanitarian activists would claim that as many as 13 million children fell into one or more of these categories, and many—like the thousands of "wolf children" (*wolfskinder*) who eked out an existence foraging in the forests and abandoned farmsteads of East Prussia and Lithuania—were survivors of forced labour camps and witnesses to horrific acts of violence. The children in Seymour's images are frequently photographed against a backdrop of urban rubble and deprivation, or as in the case of Tereska Adwentowska, living in "an institute that cares for some of Europe's thousands of 'disturbed' children." This full-page photograph struck an immediate chord with *Life*'s readership and the wider world: the surprised face of an eight-year-old Polish girl, standing beside a blackboard that is covered in a confusion of swirling, spiralling chalked lines: "Tereska [had been] asked to make a picture of her home. These terrible scratches are what she drew" (Seymour 1948, 16–17).

A larger selection of Seymour's "Children of Europe" photographs was published in book form and widely distributed by UNESCO the following year, as well as being syndicated by the Magnum agency. The impact of these photographs—like Jill Craigie's short documentary, *Children of the Ruins* (1948), *Our Children/Unzere Kinder* (Natan Gross and Shaul Goskind, 1948), Roberto Rossellini's feature film, *Germany, Year Zero/Germania anno zero* (1948), or even the illustrations by Kalman Landau included in Dorothy Macardle's important book, *Children of Europe: A Study of the Children of Liberated Countries* (1949), for example—attest both to international concerns about the plight of traumatised children and the figure of the "lost child", and the importance of film and visual culture in the discourse of post-war regeneration.[1] This was also the era in which art therapies were becoming increasingly recognised as beneficial in the treatment of mental illness, and especially in relation to the care and education of children. Some of its approaches had originated with the Bauhaus and after the war became associated with figures such as Friedl Dick-Brandeis (who had taught art to interned children in the camps at Theresienstadt and Auschwitz-Birkenau), or Adrian Hill and Edward Adamson who had introduced art therapies to various mental hospitals in England in the 1930s), while a more Jungian approach was being pioneered by child psychologists and educators in the USA, especially by Margaret Naumburg. Meanwhile in France during the 1930s and

1940s, Paul Balvet, Agnès Masson, François Tosquelles, Lucien Bonnafé and others made art therapies and the involvement of visual artists integral to institutional psychotherapy at Saint-Alban.

In approaching the educational and filmmaking methods of a figure like Fernand Deligny, a sense of this contemporary social and intellectual context is instructive. Born in 1913, he was the son of working-class parents; his father was killed fighting at the Battle of La Malmaison in 1917, and his mother was active in anarchist circles. By the late 1930s, he had left university to become a "special education" teacher, and he spent most of the war years caring for so-called "delinquent" children at a special education unit attached to the psychiatric hospital in Armentières, where he dealt extensively with the effects of infant trauma, abuse, and deprivation. While the neglect of adult psychiatric patients in France during the Occupation had amounted to "soft extermination", Sandra Alvarez de Toledo has remarked that "[o]ne of the paradoxes of the 'Moral Order' Vichy government in France during the Second World War was that it replaced the repressive policy then in place for the care of delinquent children with a policy of education" (2023, 4). Deligny took full advantage of this policy, although pernicious social attitudes and culpable examples of institutional negligence persisted regardless.

WORK AND CULTURE

Communist in his politics, Deligny's opposition to conventional approaches to the treatment of mentally ill, disturbed, and autistic or neurodiverse children was already apparent before the Second World War, and by the time he left his job at Armentières in 1943 to work as an advisor for ARSEAA (Association Régionale pour la Sauvegarde de l'Enfant, de l'Adolescent et de l'Adulte) other teaching experiences and social commitments were shaping his ideas about education. Immediately after the war, for example, he was appointed as inaugural director of the Centre d'Observation et de Dépistage (COT) du Nord, and there he initiated an open, democratic environment for around eighty adolescents, employing "untrained" care-workers and assistants from predominantly working-class and unemployed backgrounds (recruited through his trade union and French Communist Party (PCF) links). At this time, he also began publishing some of his reflections and observations: *Graine de crapule: Conseils aux éducateurs qui voudraient la cultivar/The Rogue Seed: Suggestions for Educators Wanting its Cultivation* (1945), and *Les*

Vagabonds efficacies: Ouvriers, Artistes, Révolutionnaires, Éducateurs/ Helpful Vagabonds: Workers, Artists, Revolutionaires, Educators (1947). Perhaps unsurprisingly, given his interest in the significance of autistic gestures, traces, and silences rather than conventional linguistic forms and structures, Deligny's writing style is sketchy, aphoristic—tentative—and often characterised by neologistic and inventive associations. Writing was a vital activity for him throughout his life: Alvarez de Toledo's 2007 French edition of his works "is almost two thousand pages long [and the] sheer volume can be surprising, since [his] life with autistic persons led him to shy away from treating language and the symbolic world as the main constituents of humanness" (Wiame 2016, 41–42).

By 1946, meanwhile, Deligny had changed jobs again, becoming northern regional administrator for Travail et Culture (TEC), where he further developed his interest in cinema and filmmaking, occasionally working closely with André Bazin and Chris Marker—whom he had initially contacted when looking for a screening print of *The Road to Life/Putyovka v zhizn* (Nicolaï Ekk, 1931)—the narrative of which concerns the transformation of destitute war orphans into responsible Soviet citizens, and which was loosely adapted from the writings of Anton Makarenko, whose co-operative educational theories directly influenced Deligny's pedagogic methods and arguments, especially as he embarked on his next initiative, the creation of La Grande Cordée. In 1948, along with Huguette Dumoulin (his wife at that time), Deligny secured state funding (along with the support of the PCF) for a network to help juvenile "delinquents" by facilitating placements and vocational residencies in rural and working-class communities. Chaired by the distinguished child psychologist and fellow PCF member, Henri Wallon, and based on the French Youth Hostel Network, the aims of La Grande Cordée (which took its name from a popular—if ideologically dubious—1944 mountaineering film, *First on the Rope/Premier de cordée*), were consistent with Deligny's preference for co-operative, community-based responses to the care of children and young adults. Needless to say, the prevailing approaches to disability and mental illness in France continued to be institutional, diagnostic, and medical, with especially limited scope for enlightened thinking about such matters in a society battling economic hardship and recovering from the catastrophe of war.

La Grande Cordée lost much of its state funding in 1953 and Deligny decided to leave Paris for a rural setting, arranging for several of the children already in his care to accompany him. For the next decade, this small, barely self-sufficient community pursued a somewhat nomadic existence, seeking basic accommodation—as well as local support—wherever they could find it: first, at Salzuit (Haute-Loire), before moving north of Clermont-Ferrand to Saint-Yorre, and then south to the Cévennes, before (resignedly) accepting an invitation from Jean Oury and Felix Guattari to join the psychiatric community at La Borde, and then back to the Cévennes; initially at Guattari's recently acquired—and ramshackle— property at Gourgas, before finally settling a few miles away just outside the commune of Monoblet in 1969—where Deligny was able to form a more permanent network (*reseau*) of residencies and shelters for the teen-agers and young adults now in his care. While his two-year stay at La Borde had been motivated more by pragmatism than enthusiasm, it was by no means uneventful or without significance to his subsequent career. He had known Oury from the days of La Grande Cordée (as well as his brother, Fernand, who was associated with Célestin Freinet and Raymond Fonvieille, and was soon to be at the vanguard of the institutional peda-gogy movement); since the mid-1950s, he had also been working closely with Oury's colleague and partner, Josée Manenti—who was instrumental in the production and distribution of *The Slightest Gesture/Le moindre geste* (1964–1971). Ultimately, as Dudley Andrew suggests, when it came to La Borde, Deligny could never quite "buy into its ideology, which owed a lot to Guattari's Lacanian formation [...] Deligny was contemptu-ous of psychoanalysis and of therapy in general, believing that there sel-dom was anything wrong with a human being other than the environment into which he was forced" (Andrew 2013, 230).

Although he had a lifelong interest in the cinema, it was only during his involvement in La Grande Cordée that Deligny actively began using the camera as "a pedagogic tool", as he termed it in a 1955 essay on the sub-ject, and "the archives from these years show that cameras were included in the budgets of [his] first funding applications for the network". In fact, he continued to produce improvised sequences involving the adolescents and young adults in his care throughout the 1950s, and while "none of these projects would be concluded, they remained important to La Grande Cordée and many ideas developed at this time were carried over to the making of *The Slightest Gesture*" (Miguel 2022, 22). It is also worth not-ing the extent of creative autonomy and responsibility afforded to the young people in his care during these filmmaking activities: "The camera is at the disposition of the boy in charge of the week's scheduling" (Deligny 2022a, 59). Although he would never have dreamt of using a phrase like "the participatory documentary mode," in effect that is what Deligny's educational praxis facilitated, and in a form that was genuinely inclusive and democratic.

His earlier associations with Bazin and Marker at TEC, alongside the recent publication of his novel, *Adrien Lomme* (1958), also prompted François Truffaut to approach him for advice on scripting some scenes in his own directorial feature debut, *The 400 Blows/Les quatre cents coups* (1959). The importance of Deligny's relationship with Truffaut is worth highlighting. In practical terms, Truffaut's involvement in the development of *The Slightest Gesture*, a film that took eight years to produce; and even at that, its completion required the resourcefulness and perseverance of its principal cinematographer, Manenti, as well as Jean-Pierre Daniel's editing skills and PCF connections (the film was ultimately produced and distributed by S.L.O.N., the collective co-founded by Marker in 1967). For his part, Deligny played a role in the development and production of both *400 Blows* and *The Wild Child/L'Enfant sauvage* (1970); in the case of the latter, Suzanne Schiffman, the film's scriptwriter, even travelled to Monoblet when researching the film, meeting with Deligny and one of his wards, Janmari (Fig. 4.1).

Truffaut's support for Deligny's filmmaking was not just sentimental: having once remarked that "life is neither Nazi, Communist, nor Gaullist … it is anarchistic," he may even have identified with Deligny's anarcho-communist cast of mind (De Baecque and Toubiana 1999: 274). Although Truffaut did occasionally support some left-wing causes, his motives were usually more personal than ideological; he had also written regularly for both *Cahiers du cinéma* and *Arts (lettres, spectacles)* during the 1950s (when both journals were viewed by the Left as culturally reactionary), and by the late 1960s he was promoting a film aesthetic that was increasingly conservative in form, and commercial in motivation. He may have shared Deligny's sceptical view of psychoanalysis, but he knew little about it, and although he was genuinely concerned about the education and care of children excluded from mainstream schooling, his social arguments can seem naïve and paternalistic when compared to Deligny's more radical emancipatory positions. Most significantly, however, was their differing concepts of film form, and Truffaut's preference for dramatic substance over documentary happenstance, scripts and carefully enunciated voice-over narration over silence and serendipity. All that said, as Dudley Andrew remarks: "It is a tribute to the idealism of both men that [they] stood ready to assist each other for seventeen years despite holding such

Fig. 4.1 Everyday life and learning at Monoblet (*That Kid, There/Ce gamin, là*, 1975. Renaud Victor)

different views on all the topics that brought them together" (Andrew 2013, 233). Even during the torturous production of *The Slightest Gesture*, Truffaut was consistently supportive in terms of both advice and providing some technical resources, despite his limited availability and occasional scepticism towards the whole project (Bastide 2004, 5–13).

The Great Escape

"An erratic film," according to Serge Daney, *The Slightest Gesture* is more a collectivist docu-drama than a conventional fiction film. Its narrative— also influenced by *Adrien Lomme*—revolves around an autistic teenager, Yves Guignard, who escapes from a special school with another teenager, Richard Brougére. Free from the institutional rules and routines, they explore the maquis world at their doorstep, only for Richard to fall into a maintenance hole in a derelict farm dwelling. Eventually, the daughter of a local quarry-worker (Any Durand, who also wrote the film's script) encounters Yves and returns with him to the unit, where he is reunited with the now rescued Richard. Between 1963–65, Manenti shot the film locally using a 16mm Paillard, while Deligny and Guy Aubert (formerly an orphan who had participated in La Grande Cordée) created the initial soundtrack, chiefly by recording Yves's monologues at the end of each day. Further shooting took place at La Borde before filming stalled. In 1969, Jean-Pierre Daniel (who was not involved in the original production) edited the twenty hours footage into a rough cut, with final post-production and distribution managed by S.L.O.N., where the soundtrack was also mixed by Aimé Agnel and Jean-Pierre Ruh.

What is remarkable about *The Slightest Gesture* is not just its shared "authorship" and convoluted production history, or even the Beckettian echoes in Yves and Richard's acting, but its formal distinctiveness.[2] For example, it opens with a close-up of a contemporary newspaper article concerning a bull calf that had escaped from the abattoir or slaughterhouse at La Villette in Paris, only to fall into a pit before being "saved" by some fireman (before being brought back to the abattoir, presumably). The cutting of this story is followed by the opening title sequence, which among the credits states that "Yves est Yes dans ce film," "Any est Any," etc. and even "Les Cévennes sont les Cévennes." The spectator is then introduced to Yves and Deligny "off-screen": a close shot of childish images of human figures being drawn on a paper screen and Deligny's voice briefly explaining Yves' background and present circumstances (Yves had come under his care in 1958). Yves is obscured by the white drawing sheet, but his gruff utterances are clearly audible.

This opening segment establishes the film's "erratic" aesthetic, its refusal to create an exact synchronicity between image and sound, words and meaning, fiction and documentary. While the newspaper story has a clear allegorical relation to the film's theme, so too the act of drawing signifies an alternative form of expression increasingly central to Deligny's pedagogic strategies and "mappings" of autistic gestures and movements, as he once put it: "A child's drawing is not a work of art; it is a call for new circumstances" (Sauvagnargues and Holland 2016, 178). The imprint or impression of "drawing" remains discernible in many of the images and sequences that follow: the manoeuvres of the priest's scooter (framed in long shot), or the flow of the mountain stream Yves and Richard stumble upon, or in the clay that Any's father (Numa Durand) manipulates into his sculpture of her face, or the silhouetted outlines of the bare trees, scrub and textures of the distinctive Cévennes landscape (the same world that Ruspoli had explored in *Strangers of the Earth/Les Inconnus de la terre* (1962)): "The idea of a 'cinéma de terrain' owes a lot to [Deligny]" (Daney 2022, 390). *The Slightest Gesture* portrays activities such as wandering, loitering, idling, playing, doodling and drawing as modes of communication never subordinate or inferior to spoken language or writing, while also inviting the spectator to consider the possibilities of holistic living, learning, and caring; in other words, a pedagogy rooted in our availability to circumstantial, incidental, random experience rather than a dependency on institutionalised educational or therapeutic regimes.

Once alone in his wanderings, Yves is shown repeatedly working with and manipulating bits of discarded rope and cable. There are Bressonian close-up shots of his (untied) boot laces, even a stick insect is framed entwined around a piece of string; with the presence of these lines, ligatures, connections perhaps also serving as a punning allusion to *la [grande] cordée* (Fig. 4.2).

Not surprisingly, scenarios of escape and entrapment recur throughout the film, not only when, for example, Yves attacks a barn door (which Richard locked him behind), but also in a Maya Derenesque sequence in which Any poses and tries on various hats and bonnets to a soundtrack of

Fig. 4.2 Strings and attachments (*The Slightest Gesture/Le Moindre* Geste, 1971, J-P. Daniel, F. Deligny, and J. Manenti)

city sounds, imagining herself sitting elegantly on some bustling boule-vard. This sequence is also a good example of the expressive—and often dissociative—use of sound throughout *The Slightest Gesture*, an achieve-ment due in no small measure to Yves' raucous discourse and hoarse voice, with its quotations from Catholic liturgy or Napoleonic speeches at the Battle of Austerlitz, remarks about death and money, and asylums: "The asylum is terrible". The fragmentary, random quality of Yves' utterances also reinforce Deligny's fundamental scepticism about conventional lan-guage, and how it operates to exclude other realities, and negate other ways of being. Reviewing a restored print of the film after it was screened at Cannes in 2002, Jean-Michel Frodon described it as a "poem of images and sounds [in which] the incredible voice of Yves, somewhere between delirious genius and comic genius, evokes the auditory memory of the voices of Antonin Artaud, of Michel Simon, or General de Gaulle; [it is] also a political manifesto of […] radicalism, at the same time as a real aes-thetic disruption […] a palimpsest film containing the memory of the times that witnessed its birth and rebirth, of the battles that created it, of the lives that were given to it" (2002).

Despite its protracted pre-production and Deligny's ambivalent atti-tude to the concept of "completion," *The Slightest Gesture* demonstrates clearly how filmmaking informed his broader philosophy of "careless care," and belief that the camera can be instrumental in shaping the com-munal activities and shared experiences of the group or network (Witt 2022, 24). In this context, filmmaking is also "tentative" rather than definitive, and its creative processes—however provisional and incom-plete—are what matter, and not production values, schedules, and distri-bution arrangements—hence, his preference for the term "camering" (*camérer*) to convey his concept of film as an art of making, and of being—rather than one of making art and being a film artist: "While he views [filming] as driven by intentions and an end product, camering is non-subjective, endless, about the tool and the process; in short, not about making a film-object" (Moses 2022, 12). For Deligny, the filmed images and sounds are not simply framed, recorded, edited fragments of an objec-tive reality that is waiting "out there" to be assembled into a story or adapted for a screenplay; film images and sounds also reveal a subjective perception of reality, they are simultaneously projections and representa-tions, and as such constitute an important form of mapping, tracing, and transcribing outside language. For people like Manenti and Daniel—not to mention François Truffaut—all of this must have seemed like a distinctly (if even at times, infuriating) "anti-film" position, but that would be to overlook the prismatic, often paradoxical nature of Deligny's work with neuro-diverse young people, and its extraordinary attentiveness to the significance and particularity of their gestures, utterances, movements … *les moindres gestes.*

At Monoblet, and particularly through the work of Deligny's newly established Research Group on the Proximate Milieu (Groupe de recherche sur le milieu proche), an array of Super 8 film projects were initiated, especially after figures such as Jacques Lin and Gisèle Durand Ruiz, Alain Cazuc (*Projet N.*, 1989), Caroline Deligny, and Renaud Victor became involved as "nearby presences" (*présences proches*)—Deligny's term for those volunteer carers who lived with the children and young people being cared for in the community, as opposed to providing formal supervision, monitoring, or teaching roles (which Deligny disdained).[3] Victor's relationship with Deligny began in 1971 when, after seeing *The Slightest Gesture*, he visited the community with his autistic half-brother, Charles. Victor's working-class background had been especially challenging: his father had left the family when he was still very young, and a couple of years later he moved with his mother and adoptive military father to the French colony of Dahomey, before returning to Paris as a teenager. He had a disrupted education and was working as an apprentice plumber when he enrolled to audit classes at the progressive Centre Universitaire Expérimental de Vincennes (CUEV), where—now in his mid-twenties—he became involved with some left-wing and Maoist factions. A *cinéphile* since his youth, he had also joined a workers' film collective at this time (*Cinélutte*), where he first encountered Chris Marker, and Richard Copans—another filmmaker who would also become associated with Deligny.

Exemplifying a radical, artisanal form of filmmaking that combined social engagement with formal experimentation, *The Slightest Gesture* offered a spiritual homecoming of sorts for Victor. He was intuitively sympathetic to Deligny's rejection of conventional pedagogies and therapies—"these sciences"—predicated on the production of speaking subjects, and therefore "[the] child they promise to liberate, cure, or reform is in reality a product of their scholarly, social, normative institutions" (Sauvagnargues and Holland 2016, 168). Deligny, for his part, had been planning to make a documentary film involving Janmari, the non-verbal autistic child who had been put into his care in 1967, aged twelve, and who he had already introduced to Schiffman when she was researching the script for *The Wild*

Child. An important figure for Deligny in his writings and reflections, Janmari remained with the network until his death in the early 1990s. The proposed film—which would eventually be released in 1975 as *That Kid, There/Ce gamin, là*—was envisaged by Deligny as a four-hour documentary with no voice-over commentary, a film that would not so much represent the "salvation" of a particular autistic child as convey everyday life at the community or network at Monoblet, and how it is shaped *by* nonverbal children like Janmari, and not *for* them.

RAFTS IN THE MOUNTAIN

That Kid, There was largely financed by Truffaut's production company (Les Films du Carrosse), and there is a discernible thematic correspondence between it and *The Wild Child*; Sandra Alvarez de Toledo has even commented: "Seeing both films together, in terms of their content but also their formal construction, sheds new light on the current debate on the boundaries between nature and culture, the human and the non-human" (2023, 19). For Deligny, however, *The Wild Child* was too conventionally dramatic to be instructive, even if it did illustrate the irony that Dr. Jean Itard should have been learning from the "Wild Child of Aveyron" instead of teaching him, attending to his otherness and silence rather than trying to replace it with the noise of language. While necessary and welcome, Truffaut's involvement came at a price: he insisted on a much shorter running time of ninety minutes, with Deligny providing an expository voice-over commentary throughout. He also argued against Deligny's preferred title for the film, *Radeaux dans la Montagne* (*Rafts in the Mountain*) and wanted Janmari to be its central protagonist (hence, the release title). In the end, a compromise of sorts was reached: the film was cut to ninety minutes, with Victor and Deligny including a series of sequences in which the latter speaks directly to the camera about the network. These concessions risked producing a film divided against itself, both an associative participatory-observational portrayal of the network *and* an expository-didactic showcasing of Deligny's educational practices and personality. Interestingly, the seemingly over-elaborate style of the film's preamble or prologue sequence indicates how the filmmakers avoided producing two films inside one.

That Kid, There opens with some scrolling text outlining the contemporary psychiatric description of autistic children, followed by Deligny's commentary further highlighting prevailing social and medical opinions on children like Janmari, who then features in the form of a still photograph from 1967, playing with a ball attached to a string. Letters from eminent psychiatrists are ironically superimposed on this photograph, all of which diagnose Janmari as entirely dependent, isolated, and incurable: "suffering from a severe case of encephalopathy … presenting obvious psychotic traits." This image is followed by an original artist's drawing of the hospital at Armentières, with Deligny's voice-over establishing the contrast between these modern psychiatric institutions and treatments, and the "radeaux dans la montagne" at Monoblet (or more exactly, the hamlet or parish of Graniers in the Monoblet commune). The sequence cuts back to a close-up of the photograph of Janmari, with Deligny suggesting how the child's interactions with this ball, for example, presents an opportunity to reimagine our own perception of reality, to learn from Janmari and turn our version of the real inside-out. The main credits then appear (although their black typeface makes them difficult to read against the grainy black & white photograph). The film then cuts to a montage of shots from the region: an establishing shot of two large "kissing" weather-beaten rocks; an old, disused (roofless) dwelling or chapel; a long shot of other hillside dwellings, trees, and in the background the terraced cultivation slopes familiar to the region; the sequence ending with a panoramic shot of the entire valley.

The film then cuts to an image of a hand-drawn charcoal or pencil map depicting some of these houses separated by a curving line, beneath which is the handwritten word, "Monoblet." The camera pulls back to reveal it as a map of the commune, and it also features several grid-like cruciform clusters, and seemingly random, meandering lines drawn across and between them. These clusters represent the "rafts" (*radeaux*), or "living quarters" (*aires de séjour*), where the children lived among the *présences proches*, and which were spread out around the valley (a few miles apart), with Deligny remaining at the "base camp" at Graniers. The phrase "Radeaux dans la Montagne" appears on screen. It is unclear whether this text is a description of the image being shown (the map) or in fact the film's original title. This is followed by another panoramic (re-establishing?) shot of the mountain landscape, before returning to a close shot of the map and one of the rafts indicated on it ("Le Serré") before cutting to live action footage of a small group of adults and children preparing food, washing utensils, etc. Throughout this segment of the prologue, superimposed text appears at the top of the screen summarising the distinctive approach at Monoblet. In another long take, a *présence proche* clears snow

Fig. 4.3 Fernand Deligny amongst the maps and drawings at Monoblet. (*That Kid, There/Ce gamin, là*, 1975. Renaud Victor)

and ice from an outdoor living area, followed by a scene involving cooking and sharing food as the text continues to explain the purpose of the maps, and how the children have no use for ordinary language (Fig. 4.3).

In total, this prologue segment lasts over seven minutes, and comprises scrolling text, a still photograph, voice-over commentary, an artist's drawing, live action, and landscape shots (*un montage de montagnes*), images of a hand-drawn map, superimposed quotations, diegetic, incidental, and "silent" sound; with an array of shot structures deployed throughout. As the documentary proceeds, its narrative alternates between sequences showing activities at the various "rafts", Deligny talking—always generally, and even obliquely, face obscured by low-key lighting—about the work, and in particular the importance of mapping, tracing, "transcribing", and collating these visual or graphic charts of the children's movements and gestures.[4] These "wander lines" (*lignes d'erre*)—like Janmari's interactions with the ball—are for Deligny a window into our origins, another way of being and experiencing the world (Alvarez de Toledo 2013).

The aesthetic effect of the prologue, then, is also a way of deliberately releasing the film from a familiar *verité* style and predictably instructive attitude. The narration seems voiced *at* rather than voiced *over*, just as Deligny's "reports" from the (intentionally underlit) map room at Graniers remain "detached," slightly but noticeably disconnected from the film's already fragile narrative scaffolding. Importantly, in leaving most of the film free from anything resembling conventional voice-over techniques, so that even when "the voice-over commentary overlaps with outdoor sequences, [it] never relate[s] directly to the images shown [nor does it] attempt to explain autism or speak on behalf of the children", Deligny and Victor ensured that *That Kid, There* "eschews the humanitarian impulse underlying Truffaut's push for a more expository presentation of the *tentative*" (Witt 2022, 32). In its refusal to conform to the demands of producers and audiences, the film is also coincidentally faithful to the modernist spirit of the *nouvelle vague*, and a philosphy of film that subordinates narrative coherence to formal investigation, the logical to the associative.

ROUTINES, LIMITS AND ANCHOR POINTS

Like the community at Monoblet, the Warrendale residential facility for "emotionally disturbed children" existed at the intersection between various statutory bodies (education, social work, psychiatric medicine, criminal justice); unlike it, however, Warrendale exemplified a more systematic philosophy of care, one that involved relatively conventional pedagogic strategies, alongside—less conventional—re-parenting and restraint therapies aimed at enabling the children and young people to articulate their emotions and control their anti-social behaviour. While it offered a more progressive approach than whatever was available elsewhere in the Ontario childcare system in the 1960s, ultimately it endeavoured to modify the children's ways of being, not be changed by them. Essentially, its *modus operandi* was a radical form of "family therapy", with one of booklets for staff, *Routines, Limits and Anchor Points*, stating: "If a child is to function as a human being they must participate in certain routine activities each day: they must get up, get washed and dressed, eat, go to school or engage in some type of social exchange, got to bed […] this is true for the 'normal' child; it is equally true for the emotionally disturbed child" (Brown 1971, 2). Also, unlike Deligny's project, while many of the children referred to Warrendale had complex neurodiverse or schizophrenic conditions, it was not considered an appropriate care environment for those diagnosed with severe or non-verbal autism.

Situated in Etobicoke, on the outskirts of Toronto, the facility opened in late 1965. It initially consisted of four "houses," each typically comprising: twelve children, four therapist-care staff, and one overnight supervisor. Within a few months, two further "houses" had been added, and a school annex. Managed by John L. Brown (a senior psychiatric social worker and political activist for Ontario's centre-left New Democratic Party (NDP)), and its clinical director, Dr. Martin Fischer (a child psychiatrist who specialised in play and art therapies), their methods had been attracting controversy since the late 1950s; largely because of their emphasis on therapeutic holding and the confrontational "anchor point" method, which Brown described as "an extremely flexible treatment tool [that can] tie a child in their acting out and in their emotional release, to an area that can safely take whatever pathology might reveal itself" (Brown 1971, 17).[5] Originally from South Dakota, Brown studied at the University of Chicago (at that time, a pioneering centre of social work teaching and research, with its School of Social Services associated with figures like Helen Harris Perlman, John R. Seeley, and Bruno Bettleheim). He was initially employed at St. Faith's Lodge in Newmarket, Ontario, where for over a decade he developed his innovative approaches to child therapy.

While child psychiatry and developmental psychology had also become increasingly urgent fields of research after the Second World War, serious studies on the effects of therapeutic holding and physical intervention in the treatment of disturbed and traumatised children were still thin on the ground. The treatment methods deployed at the Warrendale facility were influenced by theories associated with the problem of infantile emotional deprivation (Wallon, René Spitz), group dynamics (Fritz Redl), milieu therapy (Bettleheim), and attachment (John Bowlby), as well as those elucidating the psycho-dramatic complexities of the modern family (namely, Laing, Goffman, Bateson, and others). The "anchor point" method often precipitated physical restraint and involved one or more carers using both their arms and legs to forcibly cradle the upset child or teenager, while simultaneously allowing them to give full vent to their feelings of anger and frustration without physically hurting themselves or others. In being restrained in this way, the children were actively encouraged to express their emotions as fully—and forcibly—as possible, with a view to enabling them to develop a stronger sense of trust in "parental" constraint and thus, begin to feel more secure in their relationship with benevolent authority. In justifying this approach (which was only one aspect of the Warrendale approach), Brown stated: "Our methods have to be

Fig. 4.4 Holding therapy at Warrendale. (*Warrendale*, 1967, Allan King)

unorthodox because orthodox treatments have failed with these children" (Glassman 2017) (Fig. 4.4).

Although Brown, Fischer and the other carers involved in the Warrendale project, did not withhold tranquilizing medication from the children in their care, they were committed to replacing pharmacological interventions with more holistic and behavioural forms of child psychotherapy, insisting that therapeutic tactility and physical interaction could transform how the young people perceived therapists and social workers, creating a "safe space" for them to revisit traumatic experiences of parental/social neglect, abandonment, anxiety, and abuse, and to explore and openly discuss what might be triggering distraught responses and over-reactions to given, everyday "household" situations. Brown was eager to publicise the work at Warrendale, and this—inevitably—led to arguments with the Board. He had also become increasingly involved in the provincial political scene (he was elected as an MPP to the Legislative Assembly of Ontario in October 1967), and these activities—as much as anything, Brown believed—resulted in his sacking in June 1966.[6] More significantly, perhaps, Brown's fate may have been sealed by his enthusiastic involvement in the making of Allan King's documentary film about the facility, a film originally commissioned by CBC (Canadian Broadcasting Corporation), who then refused to broadcast it in April 1967.

Warrendale was an opportune subject for a filmmaker like King, who "on numerous occasions [...] disclosed that his formative experience of family disintegration during early childhood in the Depression influenced his lifelong filmic preoccupations" (Druick 2010, 13). Initially trained and employed by CBC (Vancouver), King's early documentaries, such as *Skidrow* (1956), *The Pemberton Valley* (1958), *A Matter of Pride* (1961), or *The Pursuit of Happiness: Beyond the Welfare State* (1962) centred on homelessness, social disintegration, poverty, and unemployment. While he would go on to have a varied career as an independent filmmaker, it was the emergent television documentary format that best suited his talents and temperament, a format that by the 1960s had of course become increasingly open to some measure of *vérité* experimentation (for example, CBC's popular 1958 series, *Candid Eye*, or its successor, the *Documentary '60* series) (Hogarth 2002, 69–80). King's films from this period offered a perspective on a social reality—especially, in relation to Vancouver's inadequate welfare provision—at odds with the progressive self-image the province was trying to project, leaving his relationship with CBC—one of the principal purveyors of that image—invariably strained.

By the end of the 1950s King had set up his own production company, A.K.A. (Allan King Associates); and although still working largely for CBC, commissions and freelance contracts at that time promised him a greater degree of editorial and creative independence and permitted him to retain the theatrical distribution rights for his films (which proved important in the case of *Warrendale*). These new working arrangements also provided him with more scope to develop a distinctive style of documentary filmmaking. For example, although *Warrendale* was originally commissioned by Patrick Watson and George Desmond for CBC, its visual style contrasts markedly with CBC's *The Disordered Mind* multi-series (1960–66, Robert Anderson Associates), which comprised conventional public service documentaries aimed at informing (and reassuring) the Canadian public about the positive role their medical and statutory bodies were playing in the treatment of severe mental illness, regardless of its more complex causes and sociology. Interestingly, the third *Disordered Mind* series was broadcast in Autumn 1966 and focused on the treatment of profoundly disturbed young people; and perhaps King had these episodes in mind when he remarked that *Warrendale* was not simply "a demonstration of treatment [...], treatment is the *modus vivendi* of the environment in which the filming occurs, but it is not the subject matter of the film" (Allan King Associates 1967: npg).

King's documentary film aesthetic was broadly consistent with contemporary Canadian and French *cinéma vérité* practices. He disliked the reportage techniques and pseudo-objectivity of Direct Cinema, and he had little interest in expository or didactic documentary modes: responding to one somewhat negative review of *Warrendale*, for example, he remarked that the film "is not and was not intended as an informational film [...] it was intended purely and simply to be a film as a work of art", by which he meant that it "communicate[d] primarily on an emotional level" (King 1967, 707). Elsewhere he was dismissive of the more contrived theatrics sometimes associated with *cinéma verité*, arguing that the documentary filmmaker has to "find a sufficient tension within a work to sustain the length of what [they] want to explore [...] But for me, it's always been about people, my fascination has always been with individual people or individual people within the group—personal actuality drama, if you will" (Blaine et al. 2002, 88–89). In conceiving of documentary as "personal actuality drama," King invested considerable time and energy into developing close relationships with both his production crew and the individuals featured in his films. Ahead of shooting *Warrendale*, for example, he spent over a month visiting the house and getting to know some of the young people and staff, before introducing them to the film's camera operator and sound engineer (Bill Brayne and Russ Heise), who then visited with him every day for a further couple of weeks. Not solely in attendance to "demonstrate the Warrendale treatment," King actively sought to integrate his filmmaking project into the everyday life of the house, rather than contriving fly-on-the-wall detachment.

In describing documentary filmmaking as "personal actuality drama," King was also asserting its role in fulfilling the democratic and civic potential of television. Two months after CBC announced its decision not to broadcast *Warrendale*, the then Controller of BBC2, David Attenborough, wrote to King explaining that it too would not be screening his film. "[It] is simply too harrowing to be broadcast to a general audience," Attenborough wrote in a letter to King, adding that "[m]any, many people would, I am sure, find it so painful that they would turn away, as I did, before the end and be deeply distressed as a result. We do not feel we can properly treat our audience in this way" (Attenborough 1967). In his response to Attenborough, King explicitly defended the film in terms of its value as a work for television:

The unique virtue of television is its capacity to involve an entire nation in a shared moment of deep involvement. It is the experience of such moments which engage national insight. *Warrendale* has this capacity to enlarge attention profoundly. It treats alienation at a level which is both inescapable and ultimately promising. This is why it is so deplorable that it be denied a television audience. (King 1967)

Despite being screened at various independent cinemas and film clubs in Toronto and London, critically acclaimed after its screening at Cannes in May 1967, and winning first prize at Montreal Film Festival in August of that year, *Warrendale* was not broadcast until 30th March 1969, when it was shown by four UK independent channels (albeit on the condition—laid down by Independent Television Authority (ITA)—that it be introduced and then followed by a studio discussion with a panel of "experts").

Warrendale was shot over a five-week period in February–March 1966, producing forty hours of footage, edited into a 100-minute production at King's London studio. Comprised of twenty "episodes" or scenes, *Warrendale* culminates in the children's reactions to the sudden death of the house cook, Dorothy, and their attendance at her funeral; a very popular figure in the house, she is described at one point in the film by the senior social worker (Walter Gunn) as "a cook-mother ... the only service staff involved in the programme", and the news of her death provokes extreme responses in some of the older children and teenagers. Although initially shaped around a "Day in the Life" structure, King readily restructured the latter parts of the film to enhance the impact of the reactions to Dorothy's death—an event that actually took place much earlier in the production schedule, a manipulation of real-time chronology that exemplifies how King's method diverges from the tenets of classic *cinéma vérité*; although it is perhaps also important not to exaggerate the nature and extent of this divergence—reality is often stranger than documentary, and as William Rothman remarks in his essay, "Eternal Vérités": "In every *cinéma vérité* moment, the filmmaker happens on a situation so sublimely poignant [...] that we can hardly believe the stroke of fortune that reveals the world's astonishing genius for improvisation" (2004, 297). Other aspects of the film also pressurised its observational mode towards fictionality and dramatized actuality.

Initially scripted by Watson and King, the film contains no commentary, interviews, title music (bar a curious wobble-effect insert during the end title sequence) or other non-diegetic elements. However, *Warrendale*'s formal austerity does not so much underwrite its observational integrity as create a blank backdrop against which personalities and conflicts emerge more vividly. While its *mise en scène* was also influenced by practical considerations (such as integrating a small crew into a confined environment, and the need to minimise intrusive hand-held shooting and cumbersome sound recording set-ups), the film is especially attentive to how the presence of the camera inevitably blurs distinctions between candid and contrived modes of behaviour, and how this affects the behaviour of the children, as well as that of their carer-therapists. Take, for example, the opening segment of the film, comprising three sequences: the children being woken up for breakfast, followed by them going to school in another building within the facility; and then a "closed" meeting between John Brown and three carers (Gunn, Terri Adler, and Maurice Flood).

The film's opening title sequence is a long aerial shot, taken from a fixed camera position on the roof of an adjacent tower block, framing Adler's car as it arrives at the centre, and pulls up outside "House Two." As if to accentuate the contrast between exterior and interior worlds, perspective and scale, the subsequent shot is hand-held and taken from inside the kitchen of the house, with a kettle (ominously) coming to the boil in the foreground and Adler visible in the background—initially, through the kitchen window—as she hurriedly enters the house, greets a colleague and throws off her coat, before the hand-held camera follows her upstairs (often out of frame, and with erratic sound quality) as she endeavours to coax some of the children out of bed, and encourage others to go down for their breakfast. The camera continues to follow Terri into one of the bedrooms, where she draws open the curtains and picks up a cup and a baby-bottle (which belongs to Iréne, a teenage girl). A radio or record-player can be heard loudly in the background (playing the Rolling Stones' "Play with Fire"), as Carol (another teenage girl) angrily resists Terri's attempts to get her out of bed. She becomes increasingly irritated by Terri and refuses to budge. This situation results in a holding session, in which Terri and Maurice force Carol out from under the blanket and hold her. At this point, Walter arrives and replaces both Terri and Maurice in holding Carol. The framing also changes from rough and unsteady medium shots of Terri and Maurice grappling with Carol, to closer shots of her, and of Walter, culminating in an extreme close-up of Carol as she appears to relax, comforted rather than contained by Walter's holding. The film then cuts to a medium shot of Walter and Terri (now downstairs) discussing whether Carol should go to school that day, followed by Walter playfully lifting Tony (a young boy, who—like Carol—will become one of the film's principal characters), followed by a very long shot of the children walking together to the school building, with Tony waving and shouting at King and his crew from a distance.

This opening segment concludes with a sequence taken from a meeting later that day involving Terri, Walter, and John Brown. The meeting focuses on Terri's management of Carol that morning and involves Brown carefully chastising Terry and warning against "the dangers of precipitous holding," advising her how to relate to Carol in a more therapeutically effective way. Although running at just over three minutes in duration, Brown is rarely out of the frame in this scene, and even a brief frontal medium close-up of Terri includes his expressive hand movements in the foreground. When Walter interjects to add support to Brown's concerns about Terri's relationship with Carol, there is no cut as the camera smoothly pans right to frame Walter in a similar medium close-up, signifying continuity and consensus (Fig. 4.5).

Throughout the sequence, which is the only one featuring Brown in the entire film, King's *mise en scène* unambiguously affirms Brown's

Fig. 4.5 John L. Brown at a meeting with some colleagues. (*Warrendale*, 1967, Allan King)

authority, his role as a mentor-manager and his centrality to the entire Warrendale project. In a later sequence, Carol and Tony are filmed with Terri and Dr. Martin Fischer (described in the titles as the facility's "Medical Psychiatric Director"). In this instance, hand-held cinematography and a general atmosphere of playfulness and informality prevails, as Fischer talks to Tony about his hometown or encourages Carol to write some letters to her family. There is a contrapuntal relation between this scene and the earlier one involving Brown: here, King seems to want his audience to see the theory being put into practice, and the beneficial effects of this novel therapy on the children—and on Terri, which is important given that the film is as much about the carers, therapists and social workers as it is about the children and young people resident in the facility.

Although King would bring his distinctive 'personal actuality drama' approach to a more controversial level in his next film, *A Married Couple* (1969), *Warrendale* demonstrates documentary filmmaking as a creative process of shaping and negotiating whatever reality it finds itself encountering, a process predicated as much on a dramatic imperative as a documentary one. (Like the Deligny films, *Warrendale* is also a valuable precursor to more contemporary documentaries on similar subjects, such as Kim Longinotto's *Hold Me Tight, Let Me Go* (2007, UK), *Who Cares About Kelsey?* (Dan Habib, 2012), *A Dangerous Son* (Liz Garbus, 2018), or even King's own final film, *EMPz 4 Life* (2006) for example.) However, within the context of the film's subject matter—and the remit of this chapter—such an approach remains problematic. Despite itself, for example, *Warrendale* reinforces stereotypical images of mentally disturbed children, and the hand-held framing and use of close shots during sequences showing their emotional outbursts, tantrums, and violence dramatizes this behaviour in ways that immediately provide the audience with a *clinical—* privileged—perspective on what is happening. There is a thin line between dramatized actuality and 'actuality drama,' and in the case of *Warrendale* everyone is performing: the therapists and psychiatrists—including, Brown—are as conscious of the filmmaker's presence as the young residents. At no point do the makers of the film hand the camera over to the young people or challenge the authority of therapy (or documentary) *per se*; on the contrary, they are there to endorse—formally, as well as politically—the therapeutic methods associated with John Brown's project.

Notes

1. It was hardly coincidental that Luis Buñuel's 1950 film, *Los olvidados/The Forgotten Ones*, which centres on the doomed lives of impoverished juveniles living in the slums of Mexico City, while unpopular in Mexico (where it was produced) went on to win the Best Director award at Cannes in 1951 and quickly attracted influential supporters in Europe, including Octavio Paz, André Bazin, and Jacques Prévert.

2. Deligny admired Beckett's theatre and acknowledged the relevance of dramaturgical silence to his own work, for example, in a 1990 piece, "What Is Not Seen (by the Self)", he remarks: "What's striking about our times is that in theatre, those who stand out … don't say anything: Samuel Beckett doesn't say anything at all and he's remarkable. What's surprising is the extent to which this marks our times […] Samuel Beckett is the best of a moment in time devoted to language, it's wonderful … if only the dialogue in cinema was Beckett's" (2022b, 237).

3. "The *présences proches*, who were neither students nor healthcare professionals, received no salary. They accepted a life of material poverty in return for the freedom and open space to reinvent life in common with the children and on the children's terms, that is, without language" (Witt 2022, 28).

4. Deleuze and Guattari make an instructive reference to the maps and wander lines in their discussion of rhizome in *A Thousand Plateaus*: "Deligny transcribes the lines and paths of autistic children by means of maps […] The lines are constantly crossing, intersecting for a moment, following one another. A line of drift intersects a customary line, and at that point the child does something not quite belonging to either one: he or she finds something he or she lost—what happened—or jumps and claps his or her hands, a slight and rapid movement—and that gesture in turn emits several lines […] It is an affair of cartography. They compose us, as they compose our map. They transform themselves and may even cross over into one another. Rhizome. It is certain that they have nothing to do with language [and] they have nothing to do with a signifier [and] they have nothing to do with a structure, Deligny invokes a common Body upon which these lines are inscribed as so many segments, thresholds, or quanta, territorialities, deterritorializations, or reterritorializations" (Deleuze and Guattari 1987, 202–3).

5. *Routines, Limits and Anchor Points* was one of any number of booklets and treatment manuals written (and published) by Brown in the 1950s and 1960s.

6. By late 1967, the Board effectively dissolved the Warrendale facility, and a new care-provider was contracted by the relevant statutory authority. "[Brown] went on to establish his own private, non-profit, charitable organization of children's camps, schools and residential homes across Canada,

the United States and Europe called 'Browndale' [and] one year after Warrendale closed, 52 of the 57 children who had been in residence there had found their way back to a John Brown-run facility" (Harris 2014).

REFERENCES

Allan King Associates [A.K.A.]. 1967. *Warrendale* [Press Pack]. Toronto: AKA.
Alvarez de Toledo, S. 2013. *Cartes et Lignes D'Erre /Maps and Wander Lines: Traces du réseau de Fernand Deligny, 1969–1979*. Paris: L'Arachnéen.
———. 2023. *Fernand Deligny: In Praise of Asylum*. Exh.cat. La Virreina Centre de la Image, Barcelona. Centre Régional d'Art Contemporain, Occitanie/ Pyrénées Méditerranée.
Andrew, D. 2013. Every Teacher Needs a Truant: Bazin and *L'Enfant sauvage*. In *A Companion to François Truffaut*, eds. Dudley Andrew and Anne Gillain. 221–241. London: John Wiley.
Attenborough, D. 1967. Letter to Allan King [BBC2 and *Warrendale*]. 7th June. BFI Collections.
Bastide, B. 2004. Correspondance François Truffaut-Fernand Deligny, 1895. *Mille huit cent quatre-vingt quinze* 42: 77–110. https://doi. org/10.4000/1895.281.
Blaine, A., S. Feldman, and P. Hardcourt. 2002. Allan King Plus Three: An Interview. In *Allan King: Filmmaker*, ed. S. Feldman, 81–97. Toronto: Toronto International Film Festival.
Brown, John L. 1971. *Routines, Limits and Anchor Points*. Ontario: Browndale.
Daney, S. 2022. *The Cinema House and the World: The Cahiers du Cinéma Years, 1962–1981*. Intro. A. S. Hamrah, trans. Christine Pichini. Boston: Semiotext(e)/MIT.
De Baecque, A., and Toubiana, S. 1999. *Truffaut: A Biography*. Trans. Catherine Temerson. New York: Alfred Knopf.
Deleuze, G., and F. Guattari. 1987. *A Thousand Plateaus: Capitalism and Schizophrenia*, trans. B. Massumi. Minneapolis: University of Minnesota Press.
Deligny, F. 2022a. What Is Not Seen (by the Self) [1990]. In *Camering: Fernand Deligny on Cinema and the Image*, intro & ed. M. Miguel, trans. S. Moses, 235–238. Leiden: Leiden University Press.
——— 2022b. The Camera, A Pedagogical Tool [1955]. In *Camering: Fernand Deligny on Cinema and the Image*, intro & ed. M. Miguel, trans. S. Moses, 57–61. Leiden: Leiden University Press.
Druick, Z. 2010. *Allan King's A Married Couple*. Toronto: University of Toronto Press.
Frodon, J-M. 2002. *The Old Place* et *Le Moindre* Geste: deux splendeurs méconnues en marge du Festival official. *Le Monde*, 22 May. https://www.lemonde.

fr/archives/article/2002/05/22/the-old-place-et-le-moindre-geste-deux-splendeurs-meconnues-en-marge-du-festival-officiel_276739_1819218.html.

Glassman, D. 2017. Canada's Documentary Essentials: *Warrendale*. *POV*. 20 April. https://povmagazine.com/documentary-essentials-warrendale/.

Harris, D. 2014. Warrendale. *Etobicoke Historical Society* [Website]. https://www. etobicokehistorical.com/warrendale.html.

Hogarth, D. 2002. *Documentary Television in Canada: From National Public Service to Global Marketplace*. Montreal: McGill-Queen's University Press.

King, A. 1967. Letter to David Attenborough [BB2 and *Warrendale*]. 27th June. BFI Collection.

Miguel, M. 2022. General Introduction. In *Camering: Fernand Deligny on Cinema and the Image*, intro & ed. M. Miguel, trans. S. Moses. 15–53. Leiden: Leiden University Press.

Moses, S. 2022. Translator's Note. In *Camering: Fernand Deligny on Cinema and the Image*, intro & ed. M. Miguel; trans. S. Moses, 9–13. Leiden: Leiden University Press.

Rothman, W. 2004. *The "I" of Camera: Essays in Film Criticism, History, and Aesthetics* (Rev. ed.). Cambridge: Cambridge University Press.

Sauvagnargues, A., and E.W. Holland. 2016. *Artmachines: Deleuze, Guattari, Simondon*. Edinburgh: Edinburgh University Press.

Seymour, D ["Chim"]. 1948. Children of Europe: David Seymour's Post-War Document. *LIFE* 25 (26). www.magnumphotos.com/newsroom/david-seymour-children-of-europe/.

Wiame, A. 2016. Reading Deleuze and Guattari through Deligny's Theatres of Subjectivity: Mapping, Thinking, Performing. *Subjectivity* 9: 38–58. https://doi.org/10.1057/sub.2015.18.

Witt, C. 2022. The Space of Care: Fernand Deligny, Renaud Victor, and the Making of *Ce gamin, là* (1975). *French Screen Studies* 22 (1): 23–43. https://doi.org/10.1080/26438941.2021.2003562.

CHAPTER 5

Psychedelics

Abstract In the post-war era, especially during the 1960s and 1970s, some psychiatrists looked to psychedelic drug therapies and the anti-authoritarian politics of the counter-culture to transform traditional classifications and treatments of mental illness. In exploring how documentary film approached the converging worlds of clinical practice and popular culture at this time, this chapter examines Louis van Gasteren's "LSD" documentaries, and how they chronicle his encounters with counter-culture figures like Timothy Leary, Bart Huges, and Simon Vinkenoog; as well as with the work of the Dutch psychiatrist, Jan Bastiaans, whose controversial LSD-assisted psychotherapeutic techniques were being used in the treatment of people suffering from Second World War-related post-traumatic stress disorder.

Keywords Experimental documentary • Psychedelic psychiatry • Counter-culture • Louis van Gasteren • Drug experience films

In recent years there has been renewed support for the use of psychedelics in the treatment of mental illness, an attitudinal change popularised by writers like Michael Pollan, whose bestselling book, *How to Change Your Mind: The New Science of Psychedelics* (2019), became the basis of a Netflix docu-series as well as being instrumental in the establishment of a "Science of Psychedelics" research centre at the University of California, Berkeley

(Anwar 2020). Unlike opioids and amphetamines, the medical use of psychedelics such as LSD (lysergic acid diethylamide) or psilocybin has often been controversial: situated precariously at the junction of psychiatry and spirituality, therapy and ideology, psychedelic drugs have struggled to shake off popular misconceptions and negative counter-cultural associations. During the post-war period, however, a considerable number of psychiatrists successfully treated patients with LSD—especially, in the USA—although by the late 1960s a combination of developments in psychopharmacological research, tighter statutory controls, and changes in the economics of the pharmaceutical industry marked a decline in its clinical use. Psychedelics were still a popular recreational drug, of course, even in the form of "enhancement microdoses," but by the 1980s and 1990s that situation changed as other new, more "bespoke", drugs became readily available. In exploring how documentary film chronicled the converging worlds of radical psychiatry and psychedelic culture, this chapter focusses mainly on the filmmaking of Louis van Gasteren, tracing his documentary forays into psychedelia and its politics of consciousness, perception, and freedom, as well as his interest in psychedelic-assisted psychotherapy in the treatment of Second World War "survivor syndrome."

WAR AND TRAUMA

Van Gasteren's career encompassed an array of artistic and cultural spheres, such as: photography, journalism, installation and techno art, sound engineering, public sculpture, Eastern mysticism, Beat poetry, and classical Jazz. His documentary filmmaking engaged with national and global issues ranging from water management and housing development in the post-war Netherlands to European economic integration, and problems in the developing world. Despite his initial training as a technician and sound engineer, his work in the 1960s did not respond to the new era of light-weight cameras and television by pursuing a modishly *vérité* style or manifesto. Even in his short commercial documentaries, he embraced an independent—essayistic—approach, one that not only eschewed the formal elegance and gentile nationalism associated with the latter years of the Dutch Documentary School, but which also integrated forms, ideas, and audio-visual experiments drawn from other contemporary arts. The subject matter of his filmmaking and other artwork (which often playfully subverts distinctions between fact and fiction, subject and object, past and present) can be quirky and surreal as well as serious, frequently moving across observational, participatory, and reflexive documentary modes.

Perhaps the defining trauma of Van Gasteren's life occurred in May 1943, during the German occupation of the Netherlands. As a member of the Resistance, he agreed to hide a German-Jewish fugitive, Walter Oettinger, in his Amsterdam apartment. These were extraordinarily dangerous times: the Nazi authorities and their Dutch collaborators were nothing if not fastidious, and there was clearly no shortage of local informants: "In the Netherlands […] the Dutch police were important to the deportation of the Jews, 75% of whom (from a total of 140,000) were murdered [which] may have been because of a 'conformist authoritarian social stance' among the police rather than any real ideological support for Nazism, but the outcome was the same" (Stone 2010, 42). Doubtless traumatised by his own desperate circumstances, Oettinger's behaviour became unpredictable and reckless, endangering not only Van Gasteren but other members of his Resistance cell, and whoever they too might have been helping (there were thousands of Jewish civilians and refugees still in hiding at this time). Accounts of what happened next vary, but it seems Van Gasteren was ordered by his superiors to kill Oettinger, which he did. The corpse was soon discovered by the Amsterdam municipal police (who treated it as a civil crime) with Van Gasteren sentenced to four years imprisonment for manslaughter: "Eight months after the war [he] was reprieved, released from prison and rehabilitated as a member of the Resistance" (Pisters 2016, 76; Renders and Veltman 2021, 120).[1]

Dealing with the psychological legacy of this experience—with what would now be termed, complex post-traumatic stress disorder (PTSD)—involved Van Gasteren in various therapies and treatments throughout the 1950s and 1960s, which was—in Amsterdam as elsewhere—also a time characterised by growing inter-generational conflict and social activism, anarchic "happenings" and psychedelic experiments (Lindner and Hussey 2014). Van Gasteren was an enthusiastic "participant observer in [the Dutch] artistic counter-culture scene in the 1960s", and as well as making films and art works that engaged directly with this milieu, he "tried everything to explore the borders of his consciousness and the frontiers of self, ranging from parachute jumping, to sensory deprivation tanks, to hashish, mescaline, and LSD" (Pisters 2016, 101). Representing this era constitutes an important strand in his documentary *œuvre*, with several of his films dealing directly with the search for personal freedom and expanded consciousness. Yet, despite his impeccable counter-cultural credentials, by 1967 Van Gasteren was in his mid-forties, and by no means indifferent to the pitfalls of psychedelic excess.

Amsterdam Underground

In the mid-1960s Van Gasteren spent several months working at Harvard's Carpenter Centre for the Visual Arts, where he made an experimental short with Robert Gardner, *Out of My Skull* (1965). Although much of Gardner's research was in visual anthropology, aspects of his filmmaking chimed with Van Gasteren's reluctance to exclude subjective experience from documentary content. *Dead Birds*, for example, Gardner's 1963 film about warrior rituals among the Dugum Dani of New Guinea, clearly—and controversially—demonstrated his sceptical attitude towards ethnographic objectivity, and the kinds of claims to authenticity made by exponents of Direct Cinema. Influenced by a suitably eclectic range of texts, including Aldous Huxley's essay, "Heaven and Hell" (1956), and Marshall McLuhan's *The Gutenberg Galaxy: The Making of Typographic Man* (1962), *Out of My Skull* incorporated stroboscopic and surround-sound effects, images of chaotic consumerism intercut with dreamlike slow-motion sequences, as Van Gasteren and Gardner tried to create an immersive experience by enveloping the audience in the hallucinogenic possibilities of the cinematic apparatus rather than through the distribution of sugar cubes laced with LSD. The film became a topic of political debate in the Netherlands where the authorities tried to ban it, especially after Van Gasteren exhibited it as a "film installation [...] at the Stedelijk Museum, sometimes with performances by Misha Mengelberg, Simon Vinkenoog and Johnny van Doorn" (Pisters 2016, 102).

These cultural figures, often associated with the so-called "Pleiners" (groups of artists, beatniks, students, and wanderers who congregated in the bars around Amsterdam's Leidseplein), would in turn soon identify with the anarchist Provo movement; as would Bart Huges, a former medical student and advocate of "trepanation" who—in January 1965—used a dentist's drill to bore a 5mm hole into his skull believing the procedure would increase his "brain blood volume" and create a "third eye", thereby inducing a permanent state of higher consciousness. Van Gasteren made a short documentary about this event (which included his interview with Huges the next day): *The Operation/De Ingreep* was subsequently released in 1979.[2] Huges, like Vinkenoog, had been a volunteer in LSD experiments carried out by the Dutch radical psychiatrist, Frank van Ree, in 1958–59 (Snelders 2023, 364–367).

Throughout the 1960s, suicide was also a recurrent theme in Van Gasteren's work: his mother took her own life several months after the death of his father in 1962 (and one of this grandfathers had also killed himself), and the following year he was deeply affected by the suicide of Hans van Sweeden, a twenty-five year old composer, poet, and actor, whose music Van Gasteren has used in his short film on post-war housing developments in the Netherlands, *All Birds Have Nests/ Alle vogels hebben nesten* (1961). *Hans: Life Before Death/ Hans: het leven voor de dood* (1983) is not only a requiem for Van Sweeden, it is also a creative inquiry into the lives affected by his death, and an unsentimental look at the bohemian worlds they inhabited in the late 1950s and early 1960s—a retrospective glance made particularly affecting in the film by Mengelberg's performance of Van Sweeden's minimalist compositions. While *Hans: Life Before Death* is careful not to medically or morally "diagnose" its subject, it nevertheless speculates—albeit wistfully, and from the vantage point of the early 1980s—on connections between war-related intergenerational trauma, adult drug use, artistic creativity, and emotional fragility. For Van Gasteren, Van Sweeden's death, like Huges's exercise in self-mutilation, seemed to symbolize not simply the consequences of a misguided confidence in the revolutionary potential of psychedelic drugs, but also how that moment in Dutch social history—the late 1950s and 1960s—had itself been shaped by the repressed histories and the unresolved traumas of the Second World War, and the violence—both actual and symbolic—of its postwar decolonisation process.

In *Hans: Life Before Death*, Van Gasteren carefully stitches together threads of Van Sweeden's life using found and archive footage (and photographs) from the 1960s as well as contemporary interviews, a technique that enables the present to comment on the past, or at least frame that past more securely within a critical perspective. This technique is also evident in *All Rebels/ Allemaal Rebellen*, his three-part television mini-series that was also produced in 1983. In one sense this is not surprising: *All Rebels* also makes extensive use of interviews, archive footage, photography, and other material that Van Gasteren had originally gathered while making *Hans: Life Before Death* (and other documentaries, especially *The Operation*). In another sense, however, these films are part of his wider post-mortem on the Netherlandic "Age of Aquarius," on those few psychedelic years that promised peace, love and freedom but often seemed to deliver only disappointment. Any lingering urge to romanticise the 1960s is further dispelled in *All Rebels* by Van Gasteren's decision to include both sympathetic interviews with leading figures of the counterculture as well as their "opposite numbers" in the judiciary and Dutch law enforcement agencies at that time.

The Dutch Beat poet, Simon Vinkenoog, was another important figure for Van Gasteren during the 1960s; before the *Out of My Skull* installation, for example, they had collaborated on short films such as *Mayday* (1963), and *Jazz and Poetry* (1964). One of the leading "Vijftigers" poets ("The Fifties Group"), Vinkenoog was a charismatic presence in Amsterdam's emerging underground scene, and he soon became instrumental in the city's reincarnation as the "Magic Apple." He was also an internationally recognised author, who famously "misbehaved" at Allen Ginsberg's First International Poetry Incarnation, an evening of Beat poetry held at London's Albert Hall on 11th June 1965. The following year, Vinkenoog organised similar poetry festivals in Amsterdam and Brussels, which included readings by the Black American surrealist poet and jazz musician, Ted Joans—who had also featured in Van Gasteren's *Jazz and Poetry*. Through his friendship with the American scientist, Steve Grof, Vinkenoog had been introduced to Timothy Leary and the *Psychedelic Review* "the journal of the Leary group, the first issue of which was published in 1963" (Snelders 2023, 366). He subsequently published a book about Leary's psychedelic theories, translated some of his writings into Dutch, and included Leary and Richard Alpert's essay, "The Politics of Consciousness Expansion" in his classic co-edited volume, *The Book of Grass: An Anthology of Indian Hemp* (Vinkenoog 1972; Andrews and Vinkenoog 1967, 208–213; 221–222).

Free Falling

Perhaps at Vinkenoog's prompting, Leary features in Van Gasteren's *There is No Plane for Zagreb/Nema Aviona Za Zagreb* (2012), a more explicitly autobiographical essay-film in which Van Gasteren explores the relations between his family history, the Amsterdam underground scene, LSD, and how he has dedicated his life to understanding reality, memory, and perception through filmmaking and art. He began work on this film in the mid-1960s, and then periodically abandoned it before it was finally "completed" and released in 2012. In the film, he—at this point approaching his ninetieth birthday—explains its "non-completion" as a consequence of the divorce from his wife, Jacqueline, and his separation their daughter, Mardou (who both appear in the original film). What then emerges is a cinematic sketchbook, an archive of sequences and places (mainly, from the period 1964–1969) "retrieved" by a present that can edit, replace, and rearrange these moments into a new version of the film but which cannot escape its original hypothesis that reality is always elusive ("nothing is what it seems"), and that the essence of existence resides in coincidence, happenstance, possibility, fortuitous events and strange encounters, in simply accepting what is lost or absent for what it is or was (hence, Van Gasteren's appropriation of a throwaway phrase he hears in a Belgrade travel agency into a mantra to live by: "Nema aviona za Zagreb").

A substantial segment of *There is No Plane for Zagreb* is dedicated to Van Gasteren's personal and cultural relationship with LSD. In keeping with his equivocal attitude to many aspects of the 1960s, his position on psychedelics is similarly complex. Initially attracted to LSD because it offered a new way of experiencing reality, and access to higher consciousness, he remarks in the film: "All my life, I wanted to show the other angles […] In how many dimensions can someone see, think and feel?" The transcendental promise of LSD is then under-cut by a sequence centering on the death of a student at Berkeley, Vernon L. Cox, who, in 1966, fell to his death from the window of his apartment block while taking copious quantities of the drug during an "Up, Up & Away" party. Van Gasteren also includes "street" scenes of Haight-Ashbury during the 1967 "Summer of Love", in which—reminiscent of the "direct" style and subject matter of Ed Pincus and David Neuman's *One Step Away* (1968, USA)—his hand-held camera tracks along a sidewalk where some hippies and "flower children" are hanging out. The film then cuts to another hand-held sequence involving Leary, driving his jeep while being filmed from the backseat, and then outside the Millbrook mansion, sitting on the front lawn, with flowers in his hair, talking into a microphone about this retreat being "the centre of the LSD religion in the United States." In the background, various people are filmed during an "LSD session," relaxing, dancing, and frolicking: turning on, tuning in, dropping out (Fig. 5.1).

The film then cuts to the US Johnston Barracks in Fürth, Germany, where Van Gasteren interviews Vernon Cox's parents. They talk about how they found out what had happened to their son, and a tape recording of him reading his poetry is played over different shots of San Francisco during 1967, including shots of people gathering on the iconic "Hippie Hill" at the bottom of Haight Street. At one point, Van Gasteren's hand-held camera even "floats" into their dead son's former bedsit, tracking his last movements and fatal fall. In contrast to this macabre *mise en scène*, the film then returns to Millbrook, as Leary shares a flower with one of the people taking LSD, before blithely casting aside the microphone: "I don't think we need machinery." The film then cuts back to the interview with Cox's parents, with his mother now describing their son's conventional,

Fig. 5.1 Timothy Leary "at the centre of the Psychedelic Revolution" in Millbrook, NY. (*There's No Plane for Zagreb/ Nema aviona za Zagreb*, 2012, Louis van Gasteren)

church-going upbring, and then back to Leary who comments (presumably in response to a question about the grief being experienced Cox's parents): "I share their grief, and I would try to help them understand why and how that could have happened in such a way that they might feel as proud of their son as if he had been an astronaut who had crashed or someone who has fallen in the line of high spiritual duty."[3] This part of the segment ends with a disconcerting "over-the-shoulder" shot as Van Gasteren closes the door on leaving Cox's apartment. The black & white palate is then replaced by Eastman colour, and an in-flight shot of clouds, an obvious visual pun that also indicates that Van Gasteren is travelling to India in search of further enlightenment on the subject of hallucinogens from the spiritual guru, Meher Baba.

Leary, and especially during his "residency" at Millbrook (1963–1968), was keen to publicise the psychic benefits of LSD and he had soon attracted a growing circle of well-known—and not so well-known—supporters who joined in "psychedelic explorations, creative writing projects, gardening, and connecting with artists, musicians, philosophers, researchers, journalists [...] Ken Kesey and his busload of Merry Pranksters arrived unannounced one day [...] Amazing feasts and celebrations took place in the extravagantly baroque mansion that we called the Big House" (Metzner

1997, 13). Inevitably, Leary was the subject of other documentaries, and most notably during the Millbrook years: for example, D. A. Pennebaker's *You're Nobody Till Somebody Loves You* (1964), and Jonas Mekas' *Report From Millbrook* (1966).[4] Like the sequences in *There is No Plane for Zagreb*, both films adhere to a personal, essay-film aesthetic. In the case of *You're Nobody Till Somebody Loves You*, for example, Pennebaker drives to Millbrook to film Leary's marriage to the model and socialite, Nena von Schlebrügge, accompanied by some artist friends and his production crew: Monte Rock III, Diane Arbus, Darlene de Sedle, Nick Proferes, Jim Desmond, and Michael Blackwood. In the throes of developing his post-Drew Associates "performance-based revision" of Direct Cinema, Pennebaker's close framing of these essentially elusive people, of a pageant of performances and masks, "hints at the estrangement of self and identity […] rather than a conclusive portrait of Leary or Von Schlebrügge, the film is a means to another end in the form of a critique of the certitudes of the journalistic practices of direct cinema" (Beattie 2011, 89–91) (Fig. 5.2).

Fig. 5.2 Louis van Gasteren recording sound in the background at an LSD party in Millbrook, NY. (*There's No Plane for Zagreb/ Nema aviona za Zagreb*, 2012, Louis van Gasteren)

In Van Gasteren's film, the image presented of Leary's psychedelic uto-pianism is similarly ambivalent. Although he is not shown to be an advo-cate of unregulated LSD use, and—if anything—Millbrook is depicted as more idyllic than orgiastic, the inclusion of an interview with Cox's par-ents and the references to their son's aspirations as a poet keep the moral questions unresolved. Indeed, Van Gasteren even affords Leary an oppor-tunity to respond to Baba's belief that genuinely divine experiences are not possible through drugs: "My way of finding my divinity is different." Ultimately, the older Van Gasteren concludes that while LSD may well be a dangerous drug when used irresponsibly and even recreationally, in ret-rospect he states: "I am sure: without LSD I would have ended my life ... just like my mother and grandfather."

Now Do You Get It Why I Am Crying?

While originally researching materials and filming *There is No Plane for Zagreb*, Van Gasteren became interested in the medicinal uses of psyche-delics, and in Jan Bastiaans' alternative psychotherapeutic (or psycholytic) treatment programme which combined psychoanalysis with the adminis-tration of drugs such as pentobarbital or sodium pentothal, and LSD: "LSD use in the Netherlands had its own characteristics [...] LSD therapy in psychiatry was closely connected to the culture of Dutch psychiatry of the time, and to the traumas and heritage of the German occupation in the Second World War" (Snelders 2023, 370). A conventionally trained psy-chiatrist who had initially embraced Freudian psychoanalysis in the late 1940s, Bastiaans completed his doctoral thesis on "psychosomatic after-effects of oppression and resistance" (Bastiaans 1957; Van Bergen 2023, 21–28). Subsequently, based at Leiden University's Jelgersma Clinic, his drug-assisted therapies were considered unorthodox by his peers but in the post-war era these treatments enjoyed some political support, and he emerged as an influential advocate for the rights of Nazi concentration camp survivors, as well as former resistance fighters, prisoners-of-war, and returning internees from Japan's wartime occupation of the Dutch East Indies (Indonesia): "In the setting of psychiatric treatment, and more spe-cifically in sessions with LSD or psilocybin, [Bastiaans] took the position of the father-figure who gave his patients the warmth and understanding they required [...] this gave him the emotional involvement needed for a successful therapeutic use of LSD, but also made him suspect among col-leagues who worked from the mindset of professional detachment" (Snelders and Kaplan 2002, 229). His treatment also involved the use of psycho-dramatic and role-play techniques, including using actual Nazi books and posters, photographs, newsreel, military music, and recordings of Hitler's speeches to "unblock" the patient's traumatic memories and enable more effective therapy. Despite his influential supporters, including war victims, Bastiaans' methods remained controversial and by the early 1980s his therapy was being increasingly criticized: while "there were dramatic improvements, the recovery in people with serious difficulties was often temporary" (Vermetten and Olff 2013). More significantly, there was a problem of style as well as substance, and by this stage in his career Bastiaans' "personality style alienated him from a more informal and democratic new generation of psychiatrists; his students and successors were not interested in continuing his method" (Snelders 2023, 363).

Initially, Van Gasteren had wanted to film Bastiaans treating Joop Telling as part of the LSD segment in *There is No Plane for Zagreb*. Profoundly traumatised by his experiences as a concentration camp prisoner, Telling was 22 years-old when arrested in 1941 (a shipyard worker and trade unionist, he had been distributing pamphlets in support of the February Strike), imprisoned, and then deported to various camps in Germany—including Sachsenhausen and Bergen Belsen—until he was "liberated" by the Soviet army in 1945. When viewing the rushes, Van Gasteren decided that this particular encounter, and the wider story of how Bastiaans was treating sufferers of "KZ [Concentration Camp]–Syndrome", would be more appropriate as the subject of a documentary in its own right, albeit one to be produced for educational purposes: *Now Do You Get It Why I am Crying*? was originally only screened within clinical psychiatric and medical research circles before a re-edited version was made for Dutch public television, and later distributed in the USA, and Germany. Initially, Van Gasteren "made a total of 6.5 hours of film from the first five sessions [and in] the end, a bit over an hour remained" (Van Bergen 2023, 46).

The film is notable for two reasons: firstly, the public screening of the re-edited version in 1972 is believed to have influenced public opinion and the Dutch government's decision not to release the Breda Three, the last remaining Nazi war criminals still imprisoned in the Netherlands (Pisters 2016, 72–73; Van Bergen 2023, 90–93); secondly, not long after Telling's death in 2000, Van Gasteren began work on a sequel, *The Price of Survival/De prijs van overleven* (2003), which explored the effects of intergenerational trauma, and how Telling's emotional suffering and obsessive behaviour affected his family. Focusing on the experiences of

Telling's widow (Dina) and the often resentful reflections of the younger of his two sons, Reiner (who is seen playing with his father in *Now Do You Get It Why I am Crying?*), *The Price of Survival* avoids the trap of taking everything Telling's family say at face value. While Van Gasteren is never unsympathetic to their situation, as David Kettler has noted: "the explanations of self and circumstances offered by the film's protagonists should be taken as documents of the situation, not as authoritative interpretations [...] the film invites a more distanced reading of its documentary meaning, and this includes careful inquiry into what is—so to speak—expressly not said, what is hidden in the dark" (Kettler 2006, 194).

Inevitably, *The Price of Survival*, like *Now Do You Get It Why I Am Crying?*, is also about Van Gasteren himself, and it presents a perspective on some of his personal motivations as a filmmaker, and the reasoning behind his subsequent disillusionment with Bastiaans' therapeutic methods. In the earlier film, for example, Telling recalls the "rule of law" that existed among the prisoners themselves, and remarks on how survival often depended on the prisoners' own administration of punishment, as opposed to that of their guards and the Nazi authorities. Telling states to the camera that the prisoners were not a homogeneous body but in fact comprised different and distinct groups, including the underground resistance that "liquidated" certain individuals: "stealing bread ... that carried the death penalty ... stealing bread from a fellow prisoner, who only had as much as you ... was simply murder. He had to die for that ... and that happened. It wasn't so difficult": a scenario and sentiment that doubtless resonated with Van Gasteren's own traumatic wartime experience.

Despite rendering its cautiously optimistic narrative in austere 16mm black-and-white, and largely eschewing voice-over and music, *Now Do You Get It Why I am Crying?* does draw on certain expressive techniques to aestheticize its subject matter (namely, this experimental—if seemingly effective—new psychedelic-assisted treatment for profoundly traumatised survivors of the Second World War and the German Occupation of the Netherlands). It also employs disruptive framing and parallel montage strategies in depicting Telling's severe emotional suffering and its impact on his life and family relations. While broadly successful in relaying a clear—if essentially, didactic—sense of Bastiaans' therapeutic methods, the film struggles to prevent its observational ambitions from lapsing into voyeurism at times, especially in its representations of the LSD-assisted therapy session itself. This formal unevenness is partly a consequence of the film's provenance (as an episode from *There Is No Plane to Zagreb*), and its different audiences (psychiatrists and mental healthcare workers, as well as a wider television viewing public). Bastiaans, for example, is allowed to assume an essentially expository role when being filmed lecturing to his students on "KZ-Syndrome"; the shots of him behind and in front of his lectern are intercut with shots of an enrapt student audience, implying that it is *his* film about *his* work, not Van Gasteren's film about the experiences of one of Bastiaans' patients. These opening sequences situate Bastiaans as an eminently rational, authority figure whose clinical practices are based on sound scientific principles not some modish faith in the healing powers of psychedelics.

In terms of its visual style, the inclusion of personal and historical photographs, as well as archive footage from the liberation of the camps, may well have been influenced by Resnais' *Night and Fog*, a film that itself had an interesting reception history in the Netherlands and was to prove "instrumental in helping to create a certain image of the war and as an adjunct to its historiography [in that country]" (Van der Knaap 2006, 147). The presence of old family photographs (especially, those of Telling as a child, and his "unhappy" parents)—like the archive footage from the camps—immediately raises questions about how the past is documented and framed, and if personal and public histories can ever be separated, especially such deeply traumatic histories (Fig. 5.3).

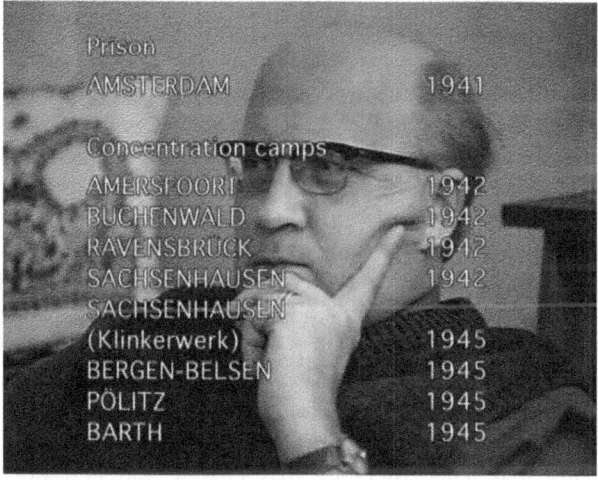

Fig. 5.3   Joop Telling, a Dutch concentration camp survivor and patient at Dr. Jan Bastiaans' clinic in Leiden. (*Now Do You Get It Why I Am Crying?/Begrijpt U Nu Waarom Ik Huil?*, 1969, Louis Van Gasteren)

For Telling, like many concentration camp survivors, the experience of the camps not only defies morality and reason but imagination itself, and his testimony leaves the audience in little doubt that a source of his present psychological turmoil is the knowledge that what happened is incomprehensible to anyone who was not there. Early in the film, for example, Van Gasteren cuts from Bastiaans' lecture (as he begins to discuss a typical case of "KZ-Syndrome") to a photograph of Telling as a young man, followed by photographs of him with his future wife, and then one from their wedding day. This montage of pre-concentration camp images is then "interrupted" by graphic archive military footage from the camps at the time of their liberation. The sequence then cuts to a contemporary scene: a long shot of Telling looking out through his large front-room window at the busy world below before a reverse shot reveals him to be watching a passing train on the other side of the street. In one sense, virtually every element in this sequence is staged—the lecture (literally), the photographs, the inclusion of archive footage, and the obvious symbolism of the train—and testifies to a documentary practice that will readily subordinate observational integrity and *directness* to rhetorical finesse and associative opportunism.

Despite its impact on wider society, the subject matter of *Now Do You Get It Why I am Crying?* no doubt challenged Van Gasteren's confidence in what documentary filmmaking can and should represent, and whether there is any point to complicating distinctions between the filmmaker as observer or participant, ethnographer or auto-biographer. Personal histories and preoccupations can ever be entirely absent from any filmmaking project, and it is worth bearing in mind that less than a year before he began work on *Now Do You Get It Why I am Crying?* Van Gasteren had accepted a commission from the Netherlands Television Service (NTS) to make a documentary about the ongoing war and famine in Biafra, *Report from Biafra/Bericht uit Biafra* (1968), with Johan van der Keuken and Roeland Kerbosch: "All three filmmakers returned shaken and devastated by the amount of misery they had seen" (Pisters 2016, 123). Ultimately, while LSD may have saved Van Gasteren, a note of pessimism is discernible in his documentary forays into psychedelics and their mind-altering possibilites. In making the *Price of Survival* some thirty-five years after the original *Now Do You Get It Why I Am Crying?*, for example, he returns—again—to a time and place of trauma in his own life, and perhaps also to the possibility that while therapies may change and new documentary images emerge, the realities of human suffering show no signs of abating.

NOTES

1. In 1990, Van Gasteren sued a daily tabloid, *Het Parool*, after it published a series of articles claiming his killing of Oettinger was in fact a premeditated murder and not a legitimate act of resistance. Although the Dutch Supreme Court found in his favour, in 1998 Van Gasteren had to take another case against a journalist who had repeated the allegations on her website. On this occasion, however, the Court found in favour of the journalist, largely because Van Gasteren had already discussed the case extensively in media interviews thereby invalidating his right to privacy in this matter (Verheij 2016, 35–36). Another Dutch journalist, Eric Slot, also investigated this incident and in 2015 he published a book questioning Van Gasteren's version of events (Slot 2015).

2. According to Stephen Snelders, Huges's attempt at self-trepanation "links the 1960s psychedelic movement to today's psychedelic renaissance: one of his followers was the noted trepanation enthusiast Amanda Feilding, whose Beckley Foundation is a major financer of today's scientific research into psychedelics" (2023, 370).

3. In 1975, a California judge ordered Leary to pay $100,000 to Cox's parents on the grounds that their son jumped to his death "while under the influence of LSD after a Leary lecture extolling the drug. Dr. Leary, now serving time concurrently for possession of marijuana and escape from prison, presented no defense to the suit brought by Hollis R. Cox, a retired Army major, and his wife, of Choctaw, Oklahoma" (Johnston 1975, 43).

4. While Mekas' "report film" centres on the local police department's raid of Millbrook, Leary "reappears" in both *Diaries Notes and Sketches* (1968), and *Walden* (1969). Joyce Wieland's *Bill's Hat* (1967) is also worth mentioning in relation to Leary's involvement with the New York avant-garde film community in the 1960s.

REFERENCES

Andrews, G., and S. Vinkenoog. 1967. *The Book of Grass: An Anthology of Indian Hemp*. New York: Grove Press.

Anwar, Y. 2020. UC Berkeley Launches New Centre for Psychedelic Science and Education. *Berkeley News*, 14th September. https://news.berkeley.edu/2020/09/14/uc-berkeley-launches-new-center-for-psychedelic-science-and-education/

Bastiaans, J. 1957. *Psychosomatische gevolgen van onderdrukking en verzet* [Psychosomatic After-Effects of Oppression and Resistance]. Amsterdam: Noord-Hollandse Uitgeversmaatschappij.

Beattie, K. 2011. *D.A. Pennebaker*. Urbana: University of Illlinois Press.

Johnston, L. 1975. Notes on People. *New York Times*, 25 January, p. 43. https://www.nytimes.com/1975/01/25/archives/notes-on-people-ford-to-name-judge-for-jersey.html

Kettler, D. 2006. Exile and Return: Forever Winter. *Journal of the Interdisciplinary Crossroads* 3 (1): 186–205.

Lindner, C., and A. Hussey. 2014. Concepts and Practices of the Underground. In *Paris-Amsterdam Underground: Essays on Cultural Resistance, Subversion, and Diversion*, ed. C. Lindner and A. Hussey, 13–19. Amsterdam: Amsterdam University Press.

Metzner, R. 1997. Introduction. In *Psychedelic Prayers and Other Meditations*, ed. T. Leary, 9 22. Berkeley, CA: Ronin Publishing.

Pisters, P. 2016. *Filming for the Future: The Work of Louis van Gasteren*. Amsterdam: Amsterdam University Press.

Renders, H., and D. Veltman. 2021. A Profusion of Perspectives: The Year in the Netherlands. *Biography* 44 (1): 119–125.

Slot, E. 2015. *Dood van een onderduiker: Louis van Gasteren en de waarheid* [The Strange Death of a Man in Hiding: Louis van Gasteren and the Truth]. Amsterdam: Querido.

Snelders, S. 2023. From Psychiatric Clinics to Magic Centre: LSD in the Netherlands. In *Expanding Mindscapes: A Global History of Psychedelics*, ed. E. Dyck and C. Elcock, 357–377. Massachusetts: MIT Press.

Snelders, S., and C. Kaplan. 2002. LSD Therapy in Dutch Psychiatry: Changing Socio-Political Settings and Medical Sets. *Medical History* 46: 221–240.

Stone, D. 2010. *Histories of the Holocaust*. Oxford: Oxford University Press.

Van Bergen, L. 2023. *Dutch Newspapers on War Victims and Their LSD-Treatment by Jan Bastiaans: From KZ-Syndrome to PTSD*. Cambridge: Cambridge Scholars' Publishing.

Van der Knaap, E. 2006. A Shock of Awakening: Mirroring *Nuit et Brouillard* in the Netherlands. In *Uncovering the Holocaust: The International Reception of Night and Fog*, ed. E. van Der Knaap, 129–148. London: Wallflower Press.

Verheij, A.J. 2016. The Right to Be Forgotten: A Dutch Perspective. *International Review of Law, Computers & Technology* 30 (1–2): 32–41.

Vermetten, E., and M. Olff. 2013. Psychotraumatology in the Netherlands. *European Journal of Psychotraumatology* 4. https://doi.org/10.3402/ejpt.v4i0.20832.

Vinkenoog, S. 1972. *Timothy Leary: Magiër. Het abz van de psychedelische avant-garde* [Timothy Leary: Magician, The ABZ of the Psychedelic Avant-Garde]. Leiden: A.W. Sijthoff's Uitgeversmaatschappij.

Appendix

Filmography: Documentary and Radical Psychiatry

1904, n.36. 1967. Napolitano, R. 35mm, b&w, 18 min. IT.

Ah, Sunflower. 1967. Klinkert, R. and Sinclair. I. 35mm, col, 29 min. NL.

Alienations/Aliénations. 2004. Bensmaïl, M., col, 105 min. FR.

All Divided Selves. 2011. Fowler, L. 16mm, b&w/col, 93 min. UK.

Anatomy of Violence. 1967. Davis, P. 16mm, b&w, 29 min. US.

Are the Poor Mad?/I poveri sono matti? 1971. Rotundi, M., 35mm, col/ b&w, 19 min. IT.

Asylum. 1972. Robinson, P. 35mm, col, 90 mins. CAN.

At Averroes & Rosa Parks/Averroès et Rosa Parks. 2024. Philibert, N., col, 143 min. FR.

Birth with Dr. R.D. Laing. 1978. Brew, H. and Pillsbury, S. 16mm, col, 57 min. NZ.

Breathing and Running. 1971. Robinson, P. 35mm, col, 18 min. CAN.

Contacts. 1989. Depardon, R. and Ikhlef, R. 35mm, col, 13 min. FR.

Crossing the Undergrowth of the Insane, with Jean Oury/Le Sous-bois des insensés: Une traversée avec Jean Oury. 2015. Deyres, M., col, 89 min. FR.

Day and Night/De jour comme de nuit. 1991. Victor, R. 35mm, col, 112 min. FR.

Deviant Majority, The: From Basaglia to Brazil. 2010. García, D., col, 34 min. IT/BRA.

Dialogues with Madwomen. 1994. Light, A. 16mm, col, 90 min. US.

D. O'Rawe, *Documentary Film and Radical Psychiatry*, https://doi.org/10.1007/978-3-031-74231-6

Did You Used to Be R.D. Laing? 1987. Shandel, T. and Tougas, K., col, 92 min. CAN.

Diviner, The/La Devinière. 1999. Dervaux, B. 35mm, col, 90 min. FR/BE.

Earth's Forgotten, The/Les inconnus de la terre. 1961. Ruspoli, M. 16mm, b&w, 35 mins. FR.

Every Little Thing /La Moindre des choses. 1996. Philibert, N. 35mm. col, 105 min. FR.

Excluded, The/Gli esclusi. 1969. Gandin, M. 16mm, b&w, 16 min. IT.

Family Life. 1971. Loach, K. 35mm, col, 108 min. UK.

Félix's Couch/Le divan de Félix. 1985. Pain, F. 16mm, col, 17 min. FR.

Fernand Deligny: Regarding a Film to be Made/Fernand Deligny, à propos d'un film à faire. 1989. Victor, R. 16mm, col/b&w, 67 min. FR.

Flight, The/Il volo. 1975. Agosti, S. 35mm, col, 31 min. IT.

François Tosquelles: The Politics of Madness/François Tosquelles: Une politique de la folie. 1989. Pain, F., Polack, J-C, and Sivadon, D., col, 54 min. FR.

Frantz Fanon: Memories from the Ayslum/Frantz Fanon, Mémoire d'Asile. 2002. Zahzah, A., b&w/col, 54 min. ALG.

Gardens of Abel, The/I Giardini di Abele. 1969. Zavoli, S. 16mm, b&w, 26 min. IT.

Hans: Life Before Death/Hans: het leven voor de dood. 1983. Van Gasteren, L. 35mm, b&w/col, 155 min. NL.

Happy Hours/Les Heures heureuses. 2019. Deyres, M., 35mm, col./b&w, 77 min. FR.

Here They Are/Eccoli/Les Voilà. 2015. Piermatti, G., Quadri, J., and Ricci, S., b&w, 16 min. IT/FR.

Hold Me Tight, Let Me Go. 2007. Longinotto, K, col. 100 min. UK.

House, A/Une maison. 2019. Auffray, J. col. 81 min. FR./SU.

How Does It Feel? 1976. Csaky, M. 16mm, col, 60 min. UK.

*I, Pierre Rivière, Having Slaughtered My Mother, My Sister, and My Brother...Moi, Pierre Rivière, ayant égorgé ma mère, ma soeur et mon frère...*1976. Allio, R. 35mm, col, 125 min. FR.

In Their Best Interests/Zur Besserung der Person. 1981. Bütler, H. 16mm, col, 100 min. CH.

*Institution, The.*1978. Breakwell, I., 16mm, col, 54 min. UK

Jaime. 1974. Reis, A. 35mm, col, 34 min. PT.

Knots. 1975. Munro, D. 35mm, col, 69 min. UK.

La Borde, or the Right to be Mad/La Borde ou le droit à la folie. 1977. Barrère, I. 35mm, col, 63 min. FR.

Life at Bonneuil/Vivre à Bonneuil. 1975. Seligmann, G. 16mm, col, 90 min. FR.

Life on the Raft/La Vie de radeau. 1997. Barbé-Mordillat, A., col, 52 min. FR.

Look at Madness, A/Regard sur la folie/ 1962. Ruspoli, M. 16mm, b&w, 53 min. FR.

Mad People to Untie/Nessuno o tutti—Matti da slegare. 1975. Agosti, S., Bellocchio, M., Petraglia, S., and Rulli, S. 35mm, b&w, 135 min. IT.

Mario Ruspoli: Prince of Whales/Mario Ruspoli, prince des baleines et autres raretés. 2011. Dauman, F., col., 76 min. FR.

Mental/Seishin. 2008. Sôda, K. 35mm, col, 135 min. JP.

Min Tanaka at La Borde/Min Tanaka à la Borde. 1986. Guattari, J. and Pain, F. 35mm, col, 24 min. BEL.

*Monkeys Like Becky/Monos como Becky.*1999. Jordà, J. and Villazán, N. 35mm, col, 97 min. SP.

Monsieur Deligny, The Helpful Wanderer/Monsieur Deligny, vagabond efficace. 2019. Copans, R., col, 100 min. FR.

No One Said a Word/Aucun d'eux ne dit mot. 2020. Lin, J., col, 44 min. FR.

Now Do You Get It Why I Am Crying?/Begrijpt U Nu Waarom Ik Huil? 1969. Van Gasteren, L. 16mm, b/w, 62 min. NL.

One Step Away. 1968. Pincus, E., and Neuman, D. 16mm, b&w, 54 min. US.

Open Door, The /La porta aperta. 1968. Gandin, M. 16mm., b&w, 18 min. IT.

Operation, The /De Ingreep. 1979. Van Gasteren, L. 16mm, b&w, 22 min. NL.

Out of My Skull. 1965. Van Gasteren, L., and Gardner, R. 16mm, col./b&w, 15 min. US/NL.

Out of the Shadows/À peine ombre. 2012. Djemaï, N., col, 87 min. FR.

Philadelphia Network, The/Philadelphia-nätverket. Foss, O. 1977. 16mm, b&w, 54 min. SWE.

Poetry of Madness, The/Follia come poesia. 1979. Mangiacapre, L. Super-8, col, 40 mins. IT.

Potential History of Francesc Tosquelles, Catalonia, and Fear/Història potencial de Francesc Tosquelles, Catalunya i la por. 2021. Sallarès, M., col, 135 min. CT.

Price of Survival, The /De prijs van overleven. 2003. Van Gasteren, L., col., 56 min. NL.

Projet N. 1979. Cazuc, A. 35mm. col, 56 min. FR.

Psychiatry and Violence. 1971. Robinson, P. 35mm, col, 24 min. CAN.

Psychiatry is Gonna Die/La psychiatrie va mourir. 1982. Doyle, H., Gourgues, C., and Morin, P. 35mm, col, 30 min. CAN.

R.D. Laing's Glasgow. 1978. McGreevy, J. 35mm, col, 51 min. CAN.

R.D. Laing in the USA. 1973. Robinson, P. 35mm, col, 23 min. CAN.

Reading Film from Knots by R.D. Laing. 1970. Lamelas, D. 16mm, b&w, 15 min. UK

*Report From Millbrook.*1966. Mekas, J. 16mm, col. 12 min. US.

San Clemente. 1982. Depardon, R. and Ristelhueber, S. 35mm, 90 min. FR.

Schizophrenia: A Disease or Just a Label?/Schizofreni: en sjukdom eller bara en etikett. 1970. Wallin, L. 16mm, b&w, 40 min. SWE.

Secret Childhood/Secrète enfance. 1978. Seligmann, G. 16mm, col, 92 min. FR.

Slightest Gesture, The /Le Moindre geste. 1971. Deligny, F., Manenti, J., Daniel, J-P. 16mm, b&w, 95 min. FR.

SPK Complex/SPK Komplex. 2018. Kroske, G., col, 111 min. GER.

Tale of the Serpent, The/La favola del serpent. 1968. Peltonen, P. 16mm, b&w, 29 min. FL/IT.

Testimony/Testimonio. 1969. Chaskel, P. 16mm, b&w, 7 min. CL.

That Kid, There/Ce gamin, là. 1975. Victor, R. 16mm, b&w, 88 min. FR.

The Trap: What Happened to Our Dream of Freedom. 2007. Curtis, A., col, 58 min. BBC.

There's No Plane for Zagreb/Nema aviona za Zagreb. 2012. Van Gasteren, L. 35mm, b&w/col, 82 min. NL.

'Til Madness Do Us Part/ Feng ai. 2013. Wang Bing., col, 227 min. CN.

Traces. 2013. Monferran, J-C., col, 60 min. FR.

Trieste on Basaglia/Trieste racconta Basaglia. 2012. Rossi, E. 53 min. IT.

Troublemakers. 1966. Fruchter, N., and Machover, R. 16mm, b&w, 54 min. US.

Turn On, Tune In, Drop Out. 1967. Clarke, R. 35mm, col, 82 min. US.

Unconscious Images/Imagens do inconsciente. 1987. Hirszman, L. 16mm, col, 205 min. BR.

Warrendale. 1967. King, A. 16mm, b&w, 67 min. CAN.

What If I Have a Lion in My Heart/Se ho un leone che mi mangia il cuor. 1977. Fago, A. 33mm, col, 45 min. IT.

What Remains of the Madness/Ce qu'il reste de la folie. 2014. Lachaise, J.,
  col, 101 min. FR.
What You See Is Where You're At. 2001. Fowler, L., col./b&w/stereo,
  24 min. UK.
Who Cares About Kelsey? 2012. Habib, D., col. 80 min. US.
You're Nobody Till Somebody Loves You. 1964. Pennebaker, D.A. 16mm,
  b&w, 12 min. US.

INDEX[1]

[1] Note: Page numbers followed by 'n' refer to notes.

The manufacturer's authorised representative in the EU is Springer
Nature Customer Service Centre GmbH, Europaplatz 3, 69115 Heidelberg,
Germany. If you have any concerns regarding our products, please
contact ProductSafety@springernature.com

Printed and bound by CPI Group (UK) Ltd, Croydon, CR0 4YY
27/04/2026
02097563-0012